Living Your Own Aloha

5 Steps to Manifesting Your Dreams

KELLY WEAVER

 FriesenPress

Suite 300 - 990 Fort St
Victoria, BC, V8V 3K2
Canada

www.friesenpress.com

Copyright © 2021 by Kelly Weaver
First Edition — 2021

ISBN
978-1-5255-8214-1 (Hardcover)
978-1-5255-8215-8 (Paperback)
978-1-5255-8216-5 (eBook)

1. SELF-HELP, PERSONAL GROWTH

Distributed to the trade by The Ingram Book Company

This book is dedicated to
My Left Ankle
You broke, so I could heal.

Foreword

We were born to manifest our dreams and desires—both big and small. And the book you're now holding in your hands, written by my long-time student and Law of Attraction coach Kelly Weaver, is a beautiful example of the manifestation of a deeply held desire.

Kelly graduated from the yearlong coaching certification offered by the Quantum Success Coaching Academy, which I founded over a decade ago, and is a current student in my Quantum Energy Mastery and Healing Room programs. Over the five years that I've known and worked with Kelly, I have continually been impressed by her commitment to her own spiritual and professional evolution. What you'll find on these pages is Kelly's unique interpretation of the universal laws of creation, which she's applied within herself to successfully manifest her ideal life in paradise.

The vision for this book came to Kelly while in meditation, as an inspiration to explain the principles of deliberate creation using the word ALOHA as an acronym—a philosophy and way of life that has great meaning to her. The net result is a clear, five-step formula for raising one's personal vibration to the frequency of love, a powerful state of being that magnetizes to us all and that we desire to manifest in our lives.

Throughout the book, Kelly shares generously and transparently about both the successes and the setbacks she encountered along her journey toward creating a more authentic and fulfilled life. And, because each chapter ends with an "Inspired Assignment" that encourages tangible and immediate action, *Living Your Own Aloha* provides readers with straightforward and practical ways to apply its wisdom.

The step-by-step practices shared throughout these pages will guide you, steadily and surely, to manifest the desires that are dear to your heart. The circumstances you are currently living are simply a reflection of the dominant vibration you've been offering, and at every moment, you have the power to raise your frequency and usher in a whole new reality.

Christy Whitman
NY Times bestselling author
CEO, and founder of the Quantum Success Coaching Academy

Contents

Introduction

"I couldn't heal because I kept pretending I wasn't hurt." ~ Kirsten Corley

I was broken. Literally. I had taken one misstep and there I lay with a dislocated and fractured left ankle. The surgeon put it back in place with two plates and eight screws and sent me home with crutches and pain meds. He assured me it would heal, and I'd be back to normal in about eight weeks. He was wrong. There would never be a "back to normal." Eight weeks?! Try eight-plus years, and counting. I am still healing. You see, the X-ray could not reveal just how broken I was emotionally, mentally, and spiritually. In fact, until I broke my ankle in the Honolulu airport on February 15, 2009, I didn't know it either.

On that day I broke my ankle, I went from victim to victor. It was the key that would free me from a prison of pain and open me up to a life of purpose.

That misstep turned out to be my *first* step—the aha moment when I awoke to my spirituality.

Months earlier, a friend had given me a copy of the book, *The Secret*. It was while I lay recuperating that I finally read it in one sitting. I discovered that I had known this secret my entire life, but I didn't know its name—the Law of Attraction.

I began to delve into everything I could find on the Law of Attraction, manifesting, energy work, and healing.

I learned that, as a result of my past trauma, I had a mountain of healing to work through. As a child of divorce, poverty, abuse and addiction, I had grown up in complete chaos. I was told that I would never amount to anything. The wounds of my childhood left my soul aching and my spirit broken. But out of that pain came *purpose*. Those stories are a part of my past; they are not my future. When I learned how to nurture and love that scared, abject little girl who lived inside me, she became the brave, worthy and deserving woman I am today!

Once I discovered that I had not simply been living by default, but I was actually a deliberate creator who could manifest any desire I wanted, my life changed almost instantly. And suddenly, I knew I wanted to inspire others to make their dreams a reality, too.

Yes, I live a beautiful life in Hawai'i!, but it didn't just happen. I turned obstacles into opportunities. I made decisions and took action. Using my five-step process and inspired assignments, I have manifested many of my desires. I will teach you how to do the same. I wrote this book so you don't have to spend one more day stuck, frustrated and fearful. You don't have to live in financial, emotional, or spiritual poverty any longer.

Living your own aloha is *not* about living in Hawai'i! It is about creating a life on *your* terms!

CHAPTER 1

Living Your Own Aloha

Aloha is a value, one of unconditional love.
It is the outpouring and receiving of the spirit. ~ Rosa Say

Did the word *aloha* jump out of the title? Is that one of the reasons you opened this book? If you answered yes, that's great! I hope so, because that was my intention. I envisioned my readers enjoying the book in various locations. Some readers sit on the beach, drink in hand, lulled by the waves that kiss the shore. Others soak up the sun as they lounge by a pool. Perhaps you're snuggled up in your favorite blanket by a warm fire in a cabin in the woods. Maybe you're sitting on your porch or lanai, sipping on a cold lemonade. Or perhaps it isn't that picturesque, and you're simply on the couch or in your favorite reading chair. It doesn't matter. Whatever setting you have chosen is how you live your own aloha.

What does it mean to live your own aloha? Most people know that the word *aloha* is used as a greeting to mean hello or goodbye. Unfortunately, the word is often thrown around like confetti, without understanding the sacredness. At the core, the definition of aloha is so much more. In fact, Hawaiians argue that there is genuinely no word in the English language that is equivalent in meaning.

I need to address the elephant in the room. This was a difficult chapter to write because aloha is not just a word or expression. Like an onion, it has layers. Aloha is a *value*. To many Hawaiians, it is a way of life. It's a lifestyle, passed from generation to generation. My friend Karen shared that some *kupuna* (elders) refuse to ever say the word to preserve its sacredness.

For most of my readers, using the word, *aloha* won't seem like a big deal. The word is internationally recognized and used by tourists alike. Before moving to Hawai'i nearly a decade ago, I would have had the same thought. I now understand, respect, and appreciate the sacredness of the word. As a "*haole*" (pronounced howl-lee: a word used to refer to a non-Hawaiian or Polynesian person, often what white people are called, sometimes derogatively), I want to be sensitive to the profound and complex meaning of the word.

If you look up the definition of *aloha* in the Hawaiian dictionary, you will not find just one word or phrase. You will find many words. In fact, its definition is about a paragraph in length. However, the one "definition" that stands out to me is *love*. Love encompasses so many other meanings of the defining words. Love is an emotion, not just a word; it is an experience. That is how I came to understand the meaning of aloha.

The day before we were set to move to Hawai'i, my in-laws threw us a luau-style farewell party. I want to be very clear; it was not at all what a traditional Hawaiian *luau* is supposed to be. There was some serious cultural appropriation that occurred, but it was never meant to be malicious; it was only ignorance on our part. I cringe when I look at the photos of my then nine-year-old daughter, dressed in a grass skirt, a dollar store lei, and drinking from a plastic pineapple cup.

As over one hundred family and friends arrived that day, we handed out plastic lei. We took pictures in the Hawaiian-themed photo booth. Most of the guests donned Hawaiian shirts or makeshift tropical attire. Pineapples took center stage as the decorations, and an enormous pig roasted by the side of the house. As the kids played on the slip-n-slide, the adults shared stories and memories of the good old days. The day faded into nightfall, and our hearts simultaneously exploded with love and broke painfully. We were saying goodbye to our family and friends, and a place we had called home for thirty-eight years. The reality was setting in; we were really moving to Hawai'i!

We had sold or donated almost everything we owned. Renters now occupied the only house my children ever knew. Twenty-seven boxes (could you downsize your life into twenty-seven boxes?) were shipped to our new apartment in Honolulu. The remaining items that we didn't know what to do with were stored in my in-laws' garage.

Shipping our cars made the most financial sense, so we decided to drive our van to the west coast. My in-laws would drive my hot, red convertible from Pennsylvania to California. It would also provide us an opportunity to visit states and landmarks that we wouldn't typically see. To this day, it has been my absolute favorite family memory. Besides our first trip to Disneyland, the highlight of the trip, by far, was whitewater rafting in the Grand Canyon, followed by a helicopter ride out of the canyon!

In California, we met up with my in-laws, who had taken a different route, and my best friend and her family, who came to help us get the cars shipped out. There were many logistics to consider. We were grateful for the help in maneuvering many moving parts. I will never forget the night we said goodbye to my in-laws. The memory still brings tears to my eyes.

The following day, when we were due to depart, our flight was delayed and eventually canceled. We were stranded in LAX, with more luggage than hands, no car, and nowhere to go if we couldn't get on a flight. I began to question why the Universe was delaying us now, when every green light up to this point seemed to confirm that this was to be our next chapter. Finally, we were able to rebook a flight, and we ran through the airport to make it just in time.

After we landed that night, and headed to the partially furnished apartment we'd only seen on Facetime, we stood and gazed at our view from the lanai for the first time. All at once, I broke down. *What the hell did I just do?* Here we were, just the four of us, in a place we had only visited twice for vacation (only once for our kids). We'd just moved six thousand miles from everyone we knew and loved. We had no family. No friends. No one to turn to but each other.

Over the next few weeks, we took turns crying. Emotions of anger, frustration, and grief surfaced often. School and work helped us meet many people, especially those who, like us, had moved from the mainland. But it was through those dark days that we were introduced to the true meaning of aloha.

I'll never forget that first moment I experienced it. As a teacher, I was required to attend two days of professional development before the students arrived on campus. We had no family or friends who could watch our children while both my husband and I needed to be at work. I was stressed beyond belief, as there was no way I could allow them to be home by themselves. I mentioned something about this to one of the administrative assistants we had quickly gotten to know. She said, "No, worries. You bring them to school. The Aunties will take good care of them."

We found friends who quickly became *'ohana*—our family. Beach parties, potlucks, and dinner parties filled our lonely days. Flowers and goodies often showed up on my desk at work (and still do). Neighbors offered a hand when they saw us moving into our condo. Whenever we needed help with anything, someone was there to provide a hand, smile, or word of encouragement. These people, and these experiences, showed me what aloha means at the core: *love*. It's given unconditionally, with the hope that you share it.

While I grew up on the East Coast and called it home for thirty-eight years, I do not miss the hustle and bustle of that lifestyle. Many times, I could walk down the street and pass people who never shared a hello, a smile, or even eye contact, for that matter. In Hawai'i, we greet people with a warm embrace and a kiss on the cheek. For an affectionate empath, I've died and gone to heaven!

Hawai'i, although one of the fifty states, in many ways, is like its own country. Hawai'i is a diverse community where everyone's identity thrives through aloha. As a result, people leave prejudice at the door. The welcome mat is out. Leave your *slippahs* (flip flops) and come inside.

When spirit spoke to me and told me to use the word aloha as a mnemonic to teach the steps to my manifestation process, I was also shown an image. There was a bright white bowl shimmering, and inside was a beautiful pink light. Suddenly, the light changed into cursive writing, spelling the word *love,* as it vibrated in a heartbeat rhythm in the bowl. In an instant, I realized spirit wanted me to use aloha because, at its essence, it means love. I interpreted this image to mean that love is the container that holds our intention to manifest all of our heart's desires. If we remember to wrap our intentions in love, we can expedite the process and become instant manifestors. Love is truly the answer!

Not everyone wants to move to Hawai'i or even vacation here. This book is not about that. You do not need to visit or move to Hawai'i to live your own aloha. If you live aloha and use love as your container, you can manifest your dream life anywhere, with everything you desire.

If I am completely honest, I don't truly understand the meaning of aloha. How could I, as a non-native, who has lived here for such a short time? I have not magically "arrived." Aloha is intentional, and not a state of being that is expected to be achieved overnight. Also, it needs effort to be sustained. This portrays my evolving relationship with aloha. Each day brings a chance to experience aloha, and I am humbled by it. *Love* is how I came to understand the meaning of aloha.

Inspired Assignment

An *Inspired Assignment* sure sounds like a code word for homework. Yes, I am assigning you homework; however, I promise this homework will inspire you to want to complete it. At the end of each chapter, I've given you a tangible process to try for yourself.

For your first assignment, grab a pen and a journal or notebook before you read any further. You'll want to record your responses to each assignment in one place. Or if you prefer, you can certainly write your responses in the book. Some of the steps in the process, you may have to repeat more than once, so having your inspired assignments all in one place will allow you to reflect on your growth.

You may be tempted to just read the entire book first; please don't do this. Read each chapter carefully and take the time to complete each inspired assignment before moving on to the next chapter. Each assignment builds on the previous one. Although I am teaching you a specific five-step manifestation process using the word *aloha*, I cover many other topics that will serve as the foundation to understanding the Law of Attraction and how to implement it into your life.

So, what are the steps? These specific five steps will be covered in their own individual chapters, but because I know you are eager, here's a preview:

> A is for Ask
> L is for Listen
> O is for Open
> H is for How
> A is for Act as If

In your journal or notebook, open it up to a fresh page. Take the next three to five minutes (or as much time as you need) and write down what your ideal life looks like. It's time to *dream big*! There are no right or wrong answers. It's okay to focus on material items if that's what you want. You are a deliberate creator and can have *anything* you desire.

What does *living your own aloha* mean to you?

CHAPTER 2

The Law of Attraction

As a man thinketh in his heart, so is he. ~ Proverbs 23:7

One of my favorite activities to do as a child was connect-the-dot puzzles. I could sit for hours, going through the books my grandfather would buy me. He initially found them for me as a fun way to learn how to count, but in retrospect, it taught me much more. Sometimes, I would accidentally skip a number or count incorrectly, and then the picture would be disjointed. As I mastered counting, I challenged myself to try harder puzzles with more intricate or detailed drawings. My favorite part was connecting that last dot to see what the entire picture revealed.

Connect-the-dot puzzles serve as a tangible way to see the whole picture. As you look back on your life and consider each line you joined, you notice how the pieces created the whole. You also notice that sometimes the lines are straight and at other times they are circuitous. That's how I began to understand my life. I began to see each line segment as an event or experience, explaining some of the pictures of my life as they came into focus. Some dots are still not connected and may never be; that's always the beauty and mystery of the Universe. Many times, when I questioned why something did or did not happen, the answer was revealed when I thought of my life as a connect-the-dot puzzle. This is how I have come to understand The Law of Attraction.

What is the Law of Attraction (LOA)? Explained simply: what you think about, you will attract into your reality—or *like attracts like*. This works for both positive and negative thoughts. Thoughts become things. Energy flows where attention goes. So, be aware of your thoughts!

The Law of Attraction is not new; it's been around since man began to walk the Earth. However, it wasn't clearly defined or labeled as such. It is documented in ancient civilizations, the Bible, and many religious groups. It became widely popular and more accessible after the release of the movie *The Secret* in 2006.

Many people struggle to understand LOA, because they want to know exactly *how* it works. No one questions the law of gravity, because we can observe gravity at work. If I drop my pen on the ground, it will fall. It's the law. Well, LOA is no different. Just because you can't see how it's working the evidence still shows up as your manifestation. Electricity is another example. How many people really know and understand how it works? We know it works when we turn the light on and it illuminates our once dark room.

Think of yourself as a magnet. As you send out each thought, you attract more of what you emit, good or bad. If you are thinking, "I'm going to be late for that meeting," the Universe interprets your request as, "Oh, she wants to be late—here's lots of traffic and every red light." Instead, it is essential to focus your thoughts on what you *do* want. The Universe is non-judgmental and non-biased. It will respond to your request in the same vibrational alignment at which you are vibrating. It speaks vibration, not language, so choose not only your thoughts carefully, but your emotions, too. It works all the time, is fair, and universal.

In February of 2009, my husband and I had just returned home from Hawai'i, where we celebrated an epic tenth wedding anniversary trip. The trip could not have been more romantic or perfect until the day we were set to depart for home. Just a few hours before boarding, I dislocated and broke my ankle in the airport!

I sobbed and cried for days, trying to figure out why this had happened to me. I was despondent. Yes, I had two beautiful, healthy daughters, a thriving teaching career, a loving husband, a supportive circle of family and friends, money in the bank, and a luxurious home which I owned. Yet, if I was being sincere, I was miserable. Following my ankle surgery, I had an epiphany: *I was not only physically broken, but spiritually and emotionally broken as well.* My soul was in crisis. That was the message I needed to wake the hell up. This physical break in my bone actually broke me in half, and it inspired me to use my gifts to help heal others.

In retrospect, I realize the Universe was trying to get my attention many other times, but I wasn't listening. By literally breaking my ankle, my spirit was finally awakened.

I had heard of the Law of Attraction, but didn't know much about it. While I was lying on the couch feeling sorry for myself, I remembered a book called *The Secret* that my friend Jay had given me. The copy had sat on the shelf for months, because I actually had forgotten about it. Within the first few pages, I was hooked. I read that book cover-to-cover in one day and my life completely changed.

Instead of wasting any more time watching movies, I dove into learning everything I could about the Law of Attraction and manifesting. The more I read, the more I realized that I was actually deliberately creating my life, and that I had attracted almost everything I wanted up to that point—I just never had a name for it. It was like those connect-the-dot puzzles. Now that I knew about the Law of Attraction, I could see how the dots were connecting in my life! It all made sense!

Until that moment, I believed everything that I had or experienced in my life were the result of coincidences or accidents. I didn't realize that the whole time, I had actually been creating everything I wanted and needed. I had unconsciously tapped into a superpower! But here's the thing: *you* possess the same power. There's no experience needed, or hoop through which you need to jump; it is accessible right now. Just turn on the faucet and watch it flow.

Once I became a conscious creator, my manifestation power hit a whole new level. I harnessed the power of the Universe and watched food, cars, money, homes, jobs, love, happiness, health, and you name it, flood my life. Now, don't misunderstand me. I didn't get everything I desired. Some of my thoughts have not become things just yet. But I trust that if they are for my highest good, they will arrive in Divine timing.

LOA is available to anyone and everyone who taps in, but you cannot manifest for someone else. You can pray for them, send them good vibes, hold space for their desires, but ultimately, because we are deliberate creators, the only life we create is our own.

Inspired Assignment

So, how do you tap into this power? How can you become a conscious, deliberate creator and effectively use LOA to manifest your heart's desires? It begins with your thoughts.

1. Become aware of your thoughts. Each day, you have as many as sixty thousand thoughts. How often are your thoughts positive? How often are they negative? Do you often complain, criticize, or judge? Are you positive, happy, and grateful? Most of us have recurring thoughts. Identify one negative recurring thought. Take that thought and pivot it to a positive affirmation. Here are some examples:

   Negative: *Ugh! I am so fat!*
   Positive Affirmation: *I am strong and healthy. I am my ideal weight.*

   Negative: *I am broke.*
   Positive Affirmation: *I am a money magnet. I am attracting money quickly and effortlessly.*

Even if you feel you are lying or faking it, the Universe doesn't speak English; it communicates with vibration. Positive affirmations are hundreds of times more powerful than negative ones and vibrate on a higher frequency. Every time you catch yourself saying something negative or complaining, use the pivoting process to get yourself back in vibrational alignment.

2. Remove the words "no" and "not" from your vocabulary. Humans tend to focus more on things they do not have instead of being

grateful for what they have right now. Many times, we indirectly ask the Universe for items we do *not* want.

Examples: "I don't want to be in debt," "I don't want my relationship to end." The Universe hears, "Give more debt," "End the relationship." So, be mindful of how often you negate your actual desire.

3. Ask for a gift: Still skeptical if LOA is real? Ask the Universe to give you a gift within the next week. Be open to *any* gift that may come your way. It doesn't have to be a tangible present. For example, a person in front of you in line at Target may allow you to go ahead of her. It could be that your neighbor stops by with some leftovers, or a child draws you a picture. When I did this exercise for myself, I got—no joke—a barely used Kate Spade purse (thanks, Allie), and a self-portrait that my friend painted of me (thanks Dan Paul). Neither of them had any idea that less than forty-eight hours earlier, I had challenged the Universe to give me a gift. Not only did I get one, but I received *two*! Never underestimate what—and how—the Universe will deliver.

Our thoughts create our reality. Whether or not you believe in the Law of Attraction, it is always working for you. Anytime you are thinking, it is working. If you are not attracting what you want in your life, simply change your thoughts to what you *do* want. The secret is out of the bag; the secret is the Law of Attraction. Think of the Universe as your own personal Genie. Ask for what you want, and the Universe will answer with, "Your wish is my command."

CHAPTER 3

Law of Vibration

If you want to find the secrets of the universe,
think in terms of energy, frequency, and vibration. ~ Nikola Tesla

My parents divorced when I was only eighteen months old. I have only ever known my parents living separately, so their divorce was not a traumatic issue for me. My dad's visitation day was Friday. After school, we would go to his house and settle in for a night of games, dinner, movies, mini-golf, or shopping. My dad loved playing cards, so he would teach me games like Crazy Eights, Twenty-One, Solitaire, Old Maid, and Go Fish. But my favorite game was the matching game. As an eight-year-old, I had a memory like a trap. I was able to find and remember pairs quickly, often beating my dad, who is super competitive. I think that's why I liked it so much. It was a game I could actually win.

The way to win the matching game, is to locate all of the identical pairs. The person with the most pairs is deemed the winner. Well, what the heck does this have to with vibration? The Universe operates in the same way: *like attracts like.*

Although most people understand the Law of Attraction, it is actually the Law of Vibration that is the first law. Vibration is the foundation in which the Law of Attraction is built upon. You see, everything in the

Universe is energy. As Bob Proctor says, "We live in an ocean of motion." Everything is vibrating and moving; nothing rests. The chair you are sitting on, my book in your hands, the tiniest grain of sand—all is energy. Each has its own frequency. Our job as deliberate creators, is to tune in to the same rhythm of our desires. We act as radios. Each day, we send out many different frequencies. If we are tuned in to the correct station, we attract what we want. If we are vibrating on a different frequency, we will likely hit static. How do we identify which frequency we are in? We tune in to our emotions.

In the manifestation process, our feelings serve as a compass, navigating us to know if we are in exact alignment with our desires. Abraham Hicks developed the Emotional Guidance Scale (excerpt from the book, *Ask and It is Given*, by Esther and Jerry Hicks), which I have outlined at the end of this chapter. It is a tool I use with my clients to help them identify the positive and/or negative emotions they are feeling around a particular situation. If you are vibrating in fear and grief, you are at the bottom of the scale and need to develop ways to raise your vibration; otherwise, like attracts like, and you will attract more fear and grief. Ideally, we want our emotions to be between one and five on the scale, because the higher we are on the scale, the closer we are to connecting with the Divine to manifest what we want.

As I was writing this chapter, the Universe decided I needed a refresher course. I had been feeling down—not depressed—just not myself. It was a rough start to the school year and I could tell I was just off. I couldn't put my finger on it. It seemed like everyone around me was feeling something very similar. I actually had a reading to see if something was going on planetarily, because I just couldn't get my vibration up. And then the Universe threw a curveball that totally plummeted me into fear.

One Saturday afternoon, my youngest complained of breast pain. As great parents (sarcasm), my husband and I totally blew her off. She had been bowling, so we figured perhaps she strained that area and pulled a muscle in her chest. The complaining went on for the next twenty-four hours, but it was intermittent, and honestly, it seemed tied to whenever she was asked to do homework or a chore. But by Sunday evening, she was inconsolable and obviously in a great deal of pain. In total exasperation, I took her to urgent care. I figured they would tell us it was nothing. It was just a pulled muscle, or her impending dreaded menstrual cycle. *Wrong!*

It wasn't until we got to urgent care that I saw her breast for the first time and I nearly lost my mind. There was obviously something *very* wrong. I was terrified (#22 on the emotional guidance scale) that perhaps we waited too long and that she would need a mastectomy. The doctor, while stymied because this was rare in a fourteen-year-old non-lactating young woman, assured me that it was just an infection. He prescribed antibiotics and gave us a few instructions to help manage the pain. I felt a huge relief that she would be okay, but now I felt like the worst mother in the world for not listening to her hours prior. I hadn't demanded she showed me her breast. I felt guilty (#21).

That night, I tried processing this with my husband. He told me that at age fourteen, she totally could have said, "Hey mom, it's not only really hurting, but it looks awful." Now, I was angry (#17). He was right! She should have communicated with us, or at least me! We try to give our daughters privacy now that they are becoming young women, but we've always told them if something is wrong with their bodies, they need to let us know ASAP.

On Monday, we all went to school as usual, but within only a few hours, my daughter was in the nurse's office in severe pain. I was worried (#14), but the nurse explained that the medicine simply didn't have enough time to take effect, and she should just go home and rest.

On Tuesday, we allowed her to stay home. She called me to say that the pain was even worse. The doctor needed to see her immediately, so in sheer terror, I drove home to get her. She should be better by now. Why was her body shutting down? I was telling myself all kinds of stories. I kept seeing in my mind's eye, a local news segment about flesh-eating bacteria that recently killed a woman.

Immediately after an examination, my daughter was whisked off to the emergency room to get an ultrasound. It looked like she had developed a breast abscess that may need to be drained. What in God's name is going on? Now, my mind was replaying the scene from *Castaway* where Tom Hanks has to knock out his abscessed tooth with the ice skate.

The ultrasound revealed something called a phlegmon, but it couldn't be drained. I was beyond frustrated (#10) at this point, because even though I didn't want them to drain an abscess, there was nothing they could do for my daughter's pain. They scheduled us to see a pediatric surgeon, hoping they may be able to drain it in a few days. Her antibiotics were changed, and they sent us on our way. No answers. More appointments. And a kid still in debilitating pain.

Over the next few days, the breast began to look better, but she was in such severe pain that we ended up in the emergency room again where they gave her morphine and ran all kinds of tests. The doctor looked at us and said, "Well, it's all excellent news. She doesn't have leukemia." *Leukemia?* What?! I hadn't even gone there mentally. The pediatric surgeon confirmed that it was a phlegmon, however, and that nothing could be drained at this stage. The bloodwork showed that the meds were working, so we could go home.

I sobbed and released every emotion inside me, and as I wiped the last tear, it *freaking hit me*! The entire time, I had been vibrating at such a low state, that no wonder I was attracting more worry, fear, and sadness. OMG! And here I was a Reiki certified Law of Attraction coach and healer. I knew I had to raise my vibration immediately.

I went into my daughter's room and gave her a Reiki session. She was crying and complained that she was in a lot of pain, but by the time I was finished with the session, she had fallen sound asleep. For the first time in almost a week, she slept the entire night.

From that moment, I chose my thoughts carefully. I pictured all of the cells in my daughter's body working to heal her. I whispered affirmations of wellness and healing to her for almost an hour. The next morning, she awoke in a lot less pain. Her breast looked normal again, and we were able to cancel her follow-up appointment.

The point of this story is not to claim to be some miraculous healer. The point is, that once I recognized the emotions I was feeling, I was able to climb up the emotional guidance scale much faster. While going from fear to guilt is only one level, the adjustment is significant. One degree makes a difference in water temperature. At 211 degrees, water boils. At 212 degrees, it turns into steam to operate a locomotive. One degree matters. If you can begin to recognize your emotions, and just climb one or two steps, you will be closer to tuning in to the frequency of your desire.

I truly believe the Universe had me grapple with this as I was about to write the chapter so that I could illustrate for you the scale in action. I was out of alignment and in an awful spin. I had forgotten, and needed the reminder, that I had a tool to easily get me to tune in to the frequency I wanted.

The Law of Vibration is the key to prompt manifestation. If you are in the vibrational match of your desire, you will attract it. It is the law. If it is not a vibrational match, your wish will be delayed. When my desire doesn't manifest quickly, I take an assessment using the following steps (I teach this in-depth in later chapters):

I know I need to:

1. Be crystal clear on what I want
2. Be open to possibilities
3. Detach from the *how*
4. Trust in Divine timing

When these steps are taken, I check my emotional compass and say, "Wait a minute, am I vibing and in alignment with the same frequency of my wish?" If my emotions are tuned in to the wrong frequency, I need to change the station. I cannot manifest if my feelings are emitting a different frequency than my desire. I then use a tool, like the emotional guidance scale, to realign. When I do this, my manifestations are fast, and sometimes even instantaneous.

Inspired Assignment

It is essential to build your own spiritual toolbox. I help my clients do this, so that when situations arise, they can quickly get themselves back into alignment. The emotional guidance scale is one such tool. Here is how you can use it if you are out of alignment:

1. Using the emotional guidance scale (below), identify your current emotion. Please do not judge yourself for the feelings; just recognize

them. It is totally okay if you are feeling fear (#22) and vibrating at the lowest level. The goal is to shift you to the next emotion on the scale. You most likely will not move quickly from twenty-two to one. Take one step at a time. Regardless of where your emotions are, you have the power, and are in control to move to the next level. Recognition is the first step.

2. Ask yourself *why* you are where you are? Again, there is no judgment. Many people believe they are never allowed to feel negative emotions in the manifestation process. I disagree. I often tell my clients (and myself), "You've got to feel it to heal it." You can speak positive phrases and affirmations all day long, but when your words don't match your vibration, you're not tuned in to the frequency of your desire. Sit with these emotions. Thank them for showing that you are out of alignment.

3. Play! I can hear you saying, "Kelly, I am a grown adult. I don't have time to play. Play is for kids." Actually, recreation is just play for adults. Playing naturally raises our vibration. Think about the kids you see on the playground. They swing, slide, laugh, and run around happily. Be that kid! When we play, we move our energetic vibrational bodies. Our focus is on the game and not the million things on our to-do list. If you don't like the word play, substitute it with activity or sport. Do something you enjoy. Sing, dance, draw, walk in the forest, go to the beach, ski, walk your dog, or play catch with your kids. During all the chaos with my daughter's health crisis, I went to a Harvest Moon Festival, where I got to play with essential oils, crystals, and tarot cards. I could feel my energy shift, and I came home grounded and optimistic (#5) that she would heal.

Emotions are our compass. Just like the matching game, your emotions must match the frequency of your desires. When you are listening to music, you are tuned in to a specific station or song because you enjoy it. Maybe you even sing along. Be the radio. Tune in to the frequency of your desires. The Universe is playing your song.

The Abraham Hicks Emotional Guidance Scale

1. Joy / Appreciation / Empowered / Freedom / Love
2. Passion
3. Enthusiasm / Eagerness / Happiness
4. Positive Expectation / Belief
5. Optimism
6. Hopefulness
7. Satisfaction / Contentment
8. Boredom
9. Pessimism
10. Frustration / Irritation / Impatience
11. Overwhelm
12. Disappointment
13. Doubt
14. Worry
15. Blame
16. Discouragement
17. Anger
18. Revenge
19. Hatred / Rage
20. Jealousy
21. Insecurity / Guilt / Unworthiness
22. Fear / Grief / Depression / Despair / Powerlessness

CHAPTER 4

"A" is for Ask

The answer is always no, unless you ask. ~ Kelly Weaver

Step One: "A" is for Ask. It may seem like an obvious first step, but there is actually a lot more to this than simply asking the Universe for your desire. The Universe will always manifest your requests; it's the law. However, that means you can also manifest things, situations, and relationships you don't want.

I met a woman at a workshop who complained that she could never find parking in her neighborhood. Her husband would often fight the neighbors over it. They finally gave up and sold the car. Magically, the very next day, several empty parking spaces appeared. Infuriated, she told me she didn't ask for this; she wanted a parking space! But by shaking her fist every day and asking, "why can't I ever find parking?" she got what she asked for.

I've identified what I believe are three essential keys to asking for what you want. They are Clarity, Vibration, and Belief.

Have you ever asked the Universe for a desire and it has not manifested? Did you ask the Universe for money and your wish wasn't delivered? Did you ask for a soul mate, a new car, or a house? Those are all beautiful desires that can manifest only when you have complete clarity.

As a former English teacher, who has graded thousands of students' essays, my number one critique was *details*. How is the Universe supposed to deliver you a car, a house, or some money, when you haven't given a single detail? That's like me walking into Nordstrom's and telling the sales lady I am looking for clothes. You know what comes next—the barrage of questions: "What type of clothes? What size, color, occasion, etc.?" If you ask the Universe for money, you may get it by finding a penny on the sidewalk. Hey, a penny is money, and you asked for money! So, don't be angry at anyone but yourself!

When you put your intention out into the Universe, you need to be crystal clear! You must articulate precisely what you want, so that the Universe can deliver that shiny brand-new red convertible Ferrari to your driveway. The devil is in the details. If you want money, how much do you want? When do you need it? Why do you need it? If you are trying to attract a soul mate, what does he or she look like? What are the physical, emotional, intellectual, spiritual qualities and characteristics you want in that person? When do you want to meet him or her? Depending on your skills and talents, you may even want to paint a picture, describe it in a journal, or find an image on the Internet or in a magazine, to hang by your bed so you see it each night as you go to bed and each day as you awake.

A friend of mine did this and attracted his wife. He wanted a blonde, blue-eyed woman who had a fun and energetic personality, and that's precisely who he attracted. He will often joke that when she drives him crazy, he only has himself to blame because he brought her into his life! It also makes me think of the 1980's movie *Weird Science*, where those horny teenage boys brought their lover to life!

The second key to asking lies in your vibration. As I mentioned in the previous chapter, think of yourself as a radio. All day long, we put out a frequency to the Universe. The energy we expend aligns with energy on that same frequency. Like attracts like, so whether good or bad, that's what we are bound to attract. If you are vibrating at a high frequency, then you will be a manifesting magnet. If you are vibrating low on the emotional guidance scale, you will attract things you don't want. The Universe is the best friend you could ever have. It will give you whatever you ask for and it doesn't judge. It merely responds to the energy frequency at which you are vibing.

After receiving my coaching certificate, I realized that I didn't have the business acumen I needed to be a successful entrepreneur. I invested in an eight-week business boot camp and *loved* my program and coach. A few months after completing the program, one of the coaches left. Based on my new credentials, I seemed to be the perfect fit, so I sent an inquiry email stating my interest in joining her company. Her terse reply informed me that it was not company policy to hire former clients, and basically *thanks, but no thanks*. Honestly, I was livid. I thought that it was the stupidest policy ever. My bruised ego and I moved forward though, and guess what? I didn't die! Nothing bad happened. It was simply, "no."

Although I've often been told no, I've also been told yes just as many times. My former colleagues accused me of being a suck-up and a favorite, because I usually got what I wanted. One day, I finally confronted my team leader, explaining that she had no idea how many times I was told no, but that it never prevented me from asking. What's the worst that can happen?

A few months later, another coach left. So, guess what I did? I sent another email. This time, I outlined why hiring a former client would be beneficial. Again, I was told no. Still not dead, obviously, because I'm writing this book. Of course, I was angry again and my ego took another hit, but life went on. I let it go and decided this was not the next opportunity for me. Actually, I totally forgot about it. Then, one day while checking Facebook, I had a private message from the coach who had rejected me—*twice*. She wanted to know if I was still interested in coaching for her program. Now, the tables were turned, and she was reaching out to *me*! At first, my heart sank. The reality was, I was unable to work for her full-time, and I assumed that's what she needed. Well, never make assumptions; she was in need of a coach who would pick up a few calls on the weekends. She said I could make my own schedule. The job was perfect, because that's all the time I could offer; I was hired right on the spot! A "no" today is not a no forever. The answer is always no unless you ask. So just ask!

Learning to ask for what I need and want has positively changed my life. I am now able to tap into my desires and make them come to fruition. I am no one special. You have this power, too. The difference between us may just be the popular limiting belief: "I'm not worthy. I don't deserve that," which prevents you from even asking. I've simply learned to speak to the Universe in the language frequency it understands. I'm crystal clear on my intentions and detach from how my desires will manifest.

Inspired Assignment

Let's practice by asking for money: remember our first key, *clarity*. I want to manifest five thousand dollars in the next thirty days. That's a good start, but *why* do you want it? Here is where you need to delve into your emotions. This part can be scary, but it's critical. Let's say you want the money, because you wish to pay off your credit card. Chances are, you feel anxious, panicked or worried, because you wish to pay off debt. You are actually most likely sending a vibration of lack, and not of desire. When you said aloud, I want to manifest five thousand dollars in thirty days, how did you honestly feel, and where did you feel it in your body? If you asked out of desperation, the Universe is going to match that desperate frequency and urgency by giving you more debt. Because, you see, even though your words stated you wanted money, your vibration told the Universe to bring more debt.

Before you write off the rest of this book and think I'm cuckoo, consider this: Think of a time when you woke up and you were late. How did the rest of your day progress? For most people, the rest of the day turns into one big disaster. You're late to work, you hit every red light, your boss is annoyed because you missed a meeting, you forgot your lunch, and so on. It's because your vibration was giving off worry, panic, and anger, and you just continued to attract those same vibes the rest of the day. When you *ask* the Universe for a desire, your body, mind, heart must all vibrate in a way that makes you feel as if you already have it (we will cover this concept further in a later chapter).

When it comes to vibration, "A" can also stand for awareness. You need to be aware of the vibration you are emitting. If you are attracting things into your life that you do not want, then you are not in vibrational alignment. You can't talk your way out of it by merely spewing positive affirmations. You need to become a positive vibrating magnet. Once you have mastered aligning your vibration, you will become a powerful manifesting magnet!

The third key in asking for your heart's desire comes down to your beliefs. Do you really believe you can have it? Most of the time, when someone is trying to manifest something, he or she will ask for an item but not *believe* that he or she will receive it. This goes hand-in-hand with key two of vibration. If you don't believe, it doesn't matter how many times, or in what tone you ask, the Universe is going to pick up on the vibration of disbelief and give you more of that. You have to *believe* that it is on its way. You can't trick the Universe, so don't even try.

I've asked the Universe for so many things over the years, even before I knew I had the power as a deliberate co-creator. Some of my desires have manifested, while others have not. I have become more aware of the reasons why some desires have come into existence while others have not ever come to fruition. Remember, you need to be careful about what you are asking the Universe for.

Recall the lady wanting a parking spot? She was asking for what she did *not* want, so be sure your desire is positive. You need to be *crystal* clear on what it is that you want, however, you must detach from *how* the desire will manifest. Trust and surrender that your order was received, and is on its way in divine timing. Visualize your desire in detail, but pay attention to how it will make you feel. How will you *feel* when your desire materializes into its tangible form? A no now isn't a no forever, although it could be. It just means there is something better awaiting you! It could also be a blessing in disguise to not receive what you want (more on that later). You can have anything you desire.

Manifesting is like playing a sport or instrument. It takes practice. Over time, you will be amazed at how quickly and effortlessly your desires become a reality. But first, you need to *ask*!

CHAPTER 5

Baking New Beliefs

When you believe it, you will receive it. ~ Kelly Weaver

My husband bakes the most amazing blueberry and apple pies. The secret is in his crust. He refuses to use any store-bought variety; in his opinion, the crust must be homemade, or don't even bother to waste your time baking. He uses the same ingredients and follows the same recipe every single time and, as a result, he gets a perfect pie in both looks and taste.

What would happen if my husband used different ingredients or didn't follow the recipe exactly? The pie would be different. Not necessarily bad, but it wouldn't be the pie we are accustomed to. As my fantastic mentor and Bikini Business coach, Vanessa Simpkins, would say, "You can't put a peach pie in the oven and expect an apple pie to pop out." This is the same with our beliefs.

How does this relate to beliefs? Well, you can't think negative thoughts and then believe that something positive or different will come about, just like you can't put a peach pie in the oven and pull out an apple one. Beliefs simply start out as a thought. Over time, and with life experiences, these thoughts turn into our beliefs. Many of us then confuse beliefs as being facts. Beliefs are not facts, and facts aren't beliefs. Beliefs become the ingredients we use to create the recipe of our lives.

There are two different types of beliefs: conscious and subconscious. Conscious beliefs are the ones we are aware of. Everyone thinks it's easier to change conscious beliefs because we are aware of them. Changing your unconscious beliefs is more difficult because—and most importantly—they run deeper and control so many aspects of our lives. Many times, we are not even aware that we have unconscious beliefs. Many of them are learned in childhood, before we have the ability to create our own beliefs. They are beliefs that we may have adopted from our parents or even our ancestors.

We are, in one way or another, a result of the children or grandchildren of the depression, who were raised in scarcity and adopted a scarcity mindset. There is no judgment here. Their beliefs were created during an economic crisis. Financial fear crippled them into believing there wasn't enough food, money, and resources to go around. That became their reality.

My great aunt was one of those women. Before she passed away, she cautioned my grandparents, who had taken care of her during a lengthy illness, to go through her home meticulously because she had hidden money throughout her home. I should also mention that my great aunt was a hoarder. There were several rooms in her house that my grandparents could barely enter because everything was piled and wedged from floor to ceiling. It was impossible to tell garbage from treasure. My grandmother almost threw away an old rusted tin with thirteen thousand dollars inside! My great aunt wasn't joking when she told them to look through *everything*. They are confident they threw money away, because there was simply too much stuff to go through. My great aunt had lived through a financial depression, yet died with literally thousands of dollars stuffed under mattresses and behind picture frames. I learned a valuable lesson from this: you can't take it with you.

I often think of my great aunt when I start freaking out about not having enough money. Then I realize that it is not *my* belief about money. I didn't live through the depression. That was her story, and my ancestors' beliefs about money. Nature shows me that there is an infinite and abundant Universe which provides all that I need and desire.

This is why I became a Law of Attraction coach. I wanted my clients to be able to tap in to the abundance the Universe has to offer. I want them to manifest everything their hearts desire. Over and over again, clients come to me with limiting beliefs, so before we can work on manifesting their dream careers, relationships, or homes, we need to uncover the beliefs that hold them back.

Meet Juliet (that's not her real name. *Side story: I wanted to name my daughter Juliet, but at the time, I was an English teacher and my husband was like, "no way are we having a daughter named Juliet when you teach English. That's totally over the top." Alas, I got to use my Shakespearean references in their middle names, instead. Anyway, I digress...back to Juliet.)* At the time that I coached her, Juliet was a teacher also, but knew that she needed to move beyond the academic classroom and share her gifts with the world's classroom. At a very young age, she realized she was clairaudient and clairvoyant; she could see and hear dead people. Her mom and grandmother also had the gift, but they were afraid of it and shut her down. By the time she was a teen, Juliet had denounced the gifts, and went on in life until the calling was so loud that she had no choice but to answer it. She eventually left teaching after a decade and decided to build her own spiritual business, helping other intuitive healers.

Before I started coaching her, Juliet was barely making three thousand a month as a teacher. She wanted to learn specific Law of Attraction processes to help her attract clients, but didn't know how to begin. She had tried gaining clients on her own, but nothing was working. Teaching had prepared her to be a good coach, but she wanted to learn how to start a side-coaching business like I had. Most people don't realize that starting a business is actually quite easy. What they don't understand is that the hardest part will actually be reprogramming their mindset and limiting beliefs.

When we began to delve into her past and looked at her money beliefs, everything began to change. Growing up, Juliet had watched her father succeed and fail over and over again with his business. Like most girls, she looked to her dad for safety and security. Dads were supposed to be the breadwinners. She would hear him complain about clients not paying him. He'd argue and fight with her mom. So, when she began to think about the viability of her own business succeeding, these flashbacks made her believe her business would be a failure, too.

It also brought up gender insecurity issues. How could Juliet, as a woman, be a successful business owner if her dad, a male, couldn't be? Society didn't seem to be on her side. She had learned that men make the majority of the money. A teacher's salary was acceptable because she was a woman, and she believed she didn't deserve to earn more.

Because her father's business had always been volatile, her mother worked four jobs just so they could pay their bills and have food on the table. Her mother was exhausted, unfulfilled, and overworked. Juliet believed that same fate was hers. She could never imagine that she could have a successful online business, work less, and earn more money than both of her parents combined. But here's the thing, she was already doing it. Twenty thousand dollars in three months was more than her parents could have dreamed of, because they allowed their limiting beliefs to create their realities.

Once we identified Juliet's beliefs around money, we worked to clear each and every single belief. On a conscious level, she knew most of them, but it was when we dug deeper, that she realized many of these beliefs were passed on to her from her parents. She had internalized in childhood, that pain of struggle. These beliefs were learned, so they could be unlearned. It was a matter of discovering them so she could reprogram new beliefs.

By the end of our coaching sessions, Juliet was making twenty thousand dollars. She continues to consistently make that and more, and she has had to put the clients she attracted onto a waiting list! She quit her full-time teaching job and started working entirely from home, working far fewer hours than she did as a teacher. And just as she did as a teacher, she is making a positive difference in her client's lives; they are transforming emotionally, mentally, and spiritually. Juliet's confidence has soared to new levels.

Initially, Juliet sought out a coach because she felt like she lacked business acumen, but she quickly realized it had nothing to do with running a business or coaching. She wasn't successful on her own because she had a poverty mindset. It was her money belief that held her back from shattering the proverbial glass ceiling.

Juliet and I had very similar stories about money. I grew up in an inner-city where poverty plagued my family and most of my friends. I remember being embarrassed in elementary school because I used the school's free lunch program. When my brother was born, my mom only worked part-time. When my stepfather lost his job, we almost had to go on welfare. I started working when I was fourteen-years-old because I needed (wanted) my own money to buy clothes, go to the movies, and shop at the mall with my friends. By the time I was sixteen, I held down three jobs that summer. Initially, these experiences shaped my beliefs about money: You have to work hard; cash is hard to come by, etc.

When I changed from a poverty mindset, to an attitude of abundance, my confidence soared. I knew I could achieve anything. I rewrote my money story, went to college and graduate school, and landed a teaching job at one of the top-paying school districts. Even now, my income continues to increase, because I know there is no glass ceiling to what I can earn. I'm modeling and teaching it to my husband and children, so they don't develop limiting beliefs around money, either.

It has resulted in a whole different attitude in my approach to dealing with people around me. I realize I don't have to hoard money as my great aunt did. My relationships have changed because I became more giving and willing to share, not just with money, but with my time and love as well. This is, perhaps, best illustrated in one of my favorite songs that our elementary students sing during school chapel service:

It's just like a magic penny,
Hold it tight, and you won't have any.
Lend it, spend it, and you'll have so many
They'll roll all over the floor.

Don't be like my great aunt. She had thousands of dollars and a house full of items that she never enjoyed. You can't take it with you. Yes, you can leave it for your children, but by doing that, you're perpetuating that there isn't enough. There's enough money to leave for them, but there's also enough for you to enjoy your abundant life, too.

Inspired Assignment

How can you change subconscious beliefs when you are not even aware that they exist? Actually, it's easier than it seems. You go *inward*. You meditate and think about the times and situations in your life when you believed something, but now realize you don't know where that belief came from. You can change those beliefs, whether they are conscious or subconscious. It may take some time and practice, but eventually, you can reprogram your mind with new beliefs.

For this exercise, you are only going to focus on one area of belief. Feel free, however, to repeat this process with other topics. Changing your beliefs allows you to manifest faster.

1. Identify one topic in which you have strong, clear beliefs. Some suggested topics are: money, career, love, relationships, weight loss, wellness, or health. Now, brainstorm and list every belief that you have around this one topic. Take as long as you need; you must try and identify each and every belief. If you think of new beliefs later on, just add them to the list.

2. Next, rewrite each of those beliefs into a positive affirmation.

   Example:

   > **Topic:** *Money*
   > **Belief:** *Money doesn't grow on trees.*
   > **Affirmation:** *There's an infinite supply of money available to me.*

3. Finally, when you awake and before you go to sleep, use a mirror and read these affirmations aloud for sixty-eight seconds. Use your smartphone as a timer, or if you Google "68 seconds," you will find a timer you can use. Just keep reading and re-reading until you reach sixty-eight seconds.

Why <u>sixty-eight seconds</u>? According to Esther and Jerry Hicks, authorities in the Law of Attraction, and featured in the movie, *The Secret,* "Within seventeen seconds of focusing on something, a matching vibration becomes activated. [...] And if you manage to stay purely focused upon any thought for as little as sixty-eight seconds, the vibration is powerful enough that its manifestation begins." Remember what I have stated over and over in this book: the Universe doesn't speak a language; it speaks frequency. Therefore, when you are purely focused on your intention, you are naturally raising your vibration to attract your desire. It's the law.

Baking your new beliefs is as easy as pie. Substitute all of the negative beliefs you have with positive ingredients. Shred old beliefs and discard them. Add and blend in new beliefs. Bake until set. Yields: 1 serving.

CHAPTER 6

Self-Worth = Net Worth

Self-worth cannot be verified by others. You are worthy because you say it is so. If you depend on others for your value, it is other-worth. ~ Wayne Dyer

A professor took a twenty-dollar bill from his wallet and offered it to his students. "Who would like this $20 bill?" he asked. Every hand raised. With that, he crumpled it up and asked the same question, "Who would like it now?" Every hand went up again. The professor then threw the crumpled bill onto the floor and stomped on it, grinding it with his shoe. "Now, who wants it?" he asked for the third time. All hands shot into the air. He explained to the students that this was a valuable lesson on self-worth. No matter what he did to that twenty-dollar bill, it never lost its worth. It was still valued at twenty dollars, no matter if he crumpled it up or crushed it into the ground.

The lesson we take away is that many times in life we are like that twenty-dollar bill. Our lives might feel like they are crumbling, and we are being pulverized into the ground, but we are human, not twenty-dollar bills. No matter what circumstances may happen to us—or around us—our worth should not (in theory) change. However, many of us allow life's circumstances to deplete our self-worth bank and to determine our value from extrinsic experiences.

What is self-worth? Self-worth differs from self-esteem, which is often raised or lowered by external tangibles like receiving awards, prizes, praise from others, or even gifts. Our sense of self-worth, however, is elevated or reduced by our experiences and how we react to them. Many of my clients struggle with limiting self-beliefs around their self-worth. They don't feel worthy or deserving. They don't feel valued. As a result, they struggle with manifesting their desires. I ask them to stop and take a long, deliberate look into the mirror. Many don't like what they see. They criticize their hair, or nose, or eyes. It's an excellent way for me to begin to measure how low their self-worth is. If this is how they feel about themselves on the surface, I know what must lie in their subconscious beliefs.

Think about net worth for a moment: our net worth is defined, in an economic sense, as assets minus liabilities. Let's apply this to self-worth. Using the same calculation, we must observe more positive characteristics about ourselves (assets) than we tally negatively (liabilities). Most of the time, clients who work with me have low self-worth and, as a result, have a low net worth. They have expressed that they want to learn how to manifest money. Yet as we begin uncovering their limiting beliefs, the one that invariably comes to the surface is the belief around being worthy or deserving of having more money. Once they release the unworthiness belief, they are astounded at how quickly abundance flows into their lives.

Building your self-worth and self-esteem is an ongoing process. You don't need to be perfect. You're not always going to love what you see in the mirror. There may be a new wrinkle or pimple that pops up. That's okay, as long as you begin to focus more on the positive qualities you see each time you look at yourself. When you start accepting that reflection, you know you are raising your self-worth vibration.

When I graduated from college with my teaching degree, I had thirteen interviews and four job offers. I was twenty-two years old with zero teaching experience. The job market in Pennsylvania at the time was saturated, so I was very fortunate to not only have that many interviews, but offers from which to choose. But a decade later, after visiting Hawai'i in 2009, I knew that I wanted to relocate. It was time to update the resume and take some serious action. I decided I wanted to leave public school, so I joined a private school placement agency. I had no doubt that I would be interviewed, and was certain that after eleven years of teaching, I'd be offered any job I wanted. Maybe that seemed like cockiness, but I was confident.

For the previous eleven years, I had been formally and informally evaluated by my administrators. Overall, the majority of my students performed either 'proficient' or 'advanced' on the annual state assessments. Anecdotally, I was a favorite teacher for many of my students, and they expressed this sentiment regularly in cards, drawings, letters, poetry, and baked goods. Parents respected and appreciated me, and I quickly developed a rapport with them. I was liked by most of my colleagues. I believed I was an excellent teacher who was making a positive difference.

My first rejection, however, was before I even began. To work with a placement agency, you must apply and be accepted. It had never occurred to me that I would be rejected at this first step. *Wrong.* I was denied. No explanation was given. How could a veteran teacher with my master's degree credentials be rejected? It was the chicken-egg syndrome. I couldn't get accepted, because I didn't have any private school experience, but I couldn't get private school experience, because I couldn't get approved by a placement agency.

I tried not to let it bother me too much. After all, teachers with a Master's degree and a high level of experience, are more expensive to hire. Perhaps I was simply too expensive, especially for private schools that typically pay less. I didn't give up, though. I had a friend who had a friend who had a friend (that's not a joke, it's a true networking story) who made some sort of connection with the agency on my behalf, and I was finally accepted. I was back in business!

I promptly uploaded all of the required documents and was feeling optimistic. My resume outlined a decade of impressive experience; my recommendation letters were glowing, and I had just earned a Master's degree with a 4.0 GPA. I chose the locations where I wanted to move— Florida, Hawai'i, and the southwest—where it was warm and there was no snow. I was packing my bags before I even hit enter.

Then I waited. And waited. No calls flooded in. No interviews busied my schedule. Finally losing patience, I called my placement agent to inquire what was wrong with my resume. I recall that she really didn't have an answer, but I did clearly hear the phrase, "you're not a fit." *Not a fit?* How could I, with all of my experience, passion, and dedication, not be a *fit?*

For the next several months, I began to question my abilities, my skills, and my worth—not only as a teacher, but as a human being. Then, it was recommended that I attend a hiring conference in Florida. I agreed, and headed to the conference. After that, my calendar populated quickly; I received interview after interview. I was back on track!

It was the last interview of the day that held the most promise. The school was in Honolulu. Although the job description was vague, I *knew* this was the one! This was my next school. *This was my job.* On March 19, (I remember the exact date, because it is my daughter's birthday), the phone rang. It was the school in Honolulu, offering to pay to fly me for an in-person interview. I interviewed a few weeks later on April 7, one day after my birthday. Within three months, on July 31, 2014, we moved to Honolulu and my dreams began coming true!

There were many times during the process when I wanted to give up. I questioned my worth; I didn't feel as though I deserved to get what I wanted. Actually, I had a belief that the Universe was somehow punishing me—though for God only knows what. Many times, rejection is actually protection. It guides our lives to what is best for our highest good.

During that hiring conference, I was interviewed by more than a dozen schools, yet I was only offered two positions. One school dragged out the process for weeks, making me believe that I had a real shot at getting the job. They conducted four interviews, including multiple phone calls and a tour of the school. At one point, I remember trying desperately to convince the headmaster why he should take a risk and hire me. He followed up that conversation with a cold, one-line email that stated I didn't get the job. I almost took one of the offers from Florida, but fortunately, I listened to my intuition and the undeniable signs that going to their school would be like jumping from the frying pan into the fire. The truth is, if I hadn't been rejected, I would never have landed my dream job in Hawai'i. In the end, if I am completely honest, Hawai'i was where I had wanted to go from the very beginning. The Universe heard my request and was working in the background the entire time. I was just too busy trying to micromanage it all.

Doors close and open for reasons. Opportunities come and go. What you need to understand clearly, is that a rejection is not a reflection of your self-worth. It is the Universe's way of having your back so that you get precisely what you want. Let's be clear, sometimes we think we know what we want, but we don't. If the door seems stuck, don't just keep banging on it. Try the next door, and the next one, until you become the right key. Keeping you locked out could be the best thing for you

Rejection is *not* personal. Once, my daughter attended a Broadway camp, and during the parent meeting, a casting director told us the same thing. Sometimes they need a five-foot-seven blonde-haired, blue-eyed girl in size six. You could be the most talented person in that room, but if you don't fit the description, you can't even audition. It's not personal. When I worked the drive-thru at Arby's as a teen, I was rejected daily. I was taught to "upsell" with every order, "Would you like to make that a large? Would you like to try a turnover?" Customers repeatedly told me no, but they didn't get angry that I tried to upsell them, and I didn't allow myself to be measured by how many turnovers I sold.

I later learned that several of the jobs that I had applied and interviewed for were actually not even possibilities. By law, they have to advertise their positions, but they already knew who they wanted to hire. It wouldn't have mattered how much experience I had, or how well I interviewed. I'd never even had a chance. If I had taken those rejections personally, and allowed it to affect my self-worth, I would have potentially missed the opportunity in Hawai'i.

Remember, the Universe is always working for our highest good and in perfect timing. The saying goes, that when the student is ready, the teacher appears. Sometimes, we need to learn lessons before we can evolve to what we *think* we need and want. In retrospect, I realize that I needed to learn some things about myself before I was ready to move to Hawai'i.

Inspired Assignment

Most of us have an inner critic who plays a huge role in our self-worth. It judges us on our appearance, job title, social status, and net worth. It is possible to turn that critic into a cheerleader, instead. By becoming aware that this is actually our ego trying to protect us, we can learn to silence this voice and raise our self-worth.

1. Examine your self-talk: How you talk to yourself reveals a lot about how much self-worth you already possess. When you speak

critically and negatively about yourself, it's time to *shut* the heck *up*. This lesson was a big one for me. I would call myself gross, fat, or lazy. Then, one day I did an inner child activity, and I realized that I would never ever in a million years talk like that to a child—or *anyone* for that matter, so why in God's name should I be talking like that to myself?! Please, please, start a new conversation with yourself. Pretend you are a four-year-old again. What would you say to that child? What would you celebrate and praise? What qualities would you admire in her or him? Next time you say something negative to yourself, *stop*. Instead, pivot it into a positive and loving affirmation.

2. Make a list of your capabilities and strengths. What are you good at? What are those strengths? Many times, we dwell so much on what we *can't* do that we forget about the fantastic things that we *can* do, and are probably already doing. Don't be shy or humble when itemizing these. List everything and anything that you do well. Oh, and do not judge or second-guess yourself. I can just see some of you writing this and quickly questioning, or scratching something off the list. If you are one of these people, go back to step one and start a new conversation with yourself.

3. Stop comparing yourself to others. This is hard, I know. But "comparison is the thief of joy." I ran a half marathon years ago. When the gun went off, I freaked out because people bolted and took off abruptly. At first, I tried to keep up, but I had to remind myself that I was running this race for myself. My personal goals were to finish in under three hours, and to run the entire time. I was able to accomplish both of those goals. If I had been comparing myself to the other runners around me, I would have never made it to the finish line.

Think of self-worth as an emotional piggy bank. You must take the time to make deposits into your account. Be sure to analyze your statements regularly to ensure that you are balanced. This account will never go bankrupt if you invest in yourself. *You are worth it!*

CHAPTER 7

Decision Making 101: Investing in YOU

Invest in yourself. You can afford it. Trust me. ~ Rashon Carraway

Many people thought that my taking Latin for five years would be a useless waste of time. "Latin's a dead language; no one speaks Latin. You should take Spanish. When will you ever use it?" I was an English major, so taking Latin proved to be beneficial in many ways. As I was about to write this chapter, I remembered a vocabulary lesson that my teacher taught us (shout out to Mrs. Naffin) that can actually apply to manifesting.

Each week, we would learn ten new vocabulary words. Mrs. Naffin made flashcards with pictures on them. I never had to study for her quizzes, because she would connect the image to the name by telling us a story. During the quiz, I would imagine the picture and instantly know the Latin word associated with it.

One week, our Latin word was "*decidere*," meaning to decide, determine, or literally, "to cut off." The root "*caedo*" is a very strong word, and its related noun form, "*caedes*," means "a cutting down," "killing," or "slaughter." While our word "decide" is not quite so violent, its Latin origin is. Fortunately, most decisions we will ever have to make are not life or death. The literal translation is "to cut off all possibilities." This applies to manifesting, because when we cut off all other possibilities, we are able to make a decision that the Universe can respond to.

Making decisions, especially when it comes to personal investment, often proves to be a significant block for many of my clients. Their major concern usually centers around how they will make their money back. Those beliefs come from distrusting their ability to make good decisions, or not feeling worthy of investing in themselves. As a result, they allow fear to chain them into complacency. Eventually, those restraints either keep them imprisoned in the safety of indecision, or must be broken to free them.

Once upon a time, I was a terrible decision-maker. I waffled on *every* decision I needed to make. It didn't matter how big or small the decision was, I would be paralyzed in fear of making the wrong choice. So, for much of my life, I chose what I knew, what was easy, or what was comfortable. I didn't dare sample a new dish at a restaurant, or even try on a dress with a pattern. It's actually ridiculous when I think about it, but decision making, for me, was tied to a lack of trust and confidence in myself. For many years, I grappled with self-esteem and self-worth issues. Fortunately, when I became spiritually awakened, I realized that if I didn't begin to make decisions swiftly and intuitively, I was never going to manifest the life I wanted. If you're going to be a master manifestor, you must become a master at making decisions.

It was in 2015 that I learned about a Law of Attraction coaching certification program called *The Quantum Success Academy*. At that time, they were offering free coaching sessions with current students in the program. I figured this would be a great way to get an inside look at the program. They matched me up with a male coach, and a few weeks later, we had our first free call. I'm not going to lie. It was terrible. His internet access was spotty at best, so the call cut in and out. For much of the call, I couldn't hear him, and it felt like I was in a real-life commercial of "Can you hear me? Can you hear me now?" After providing this feedback, the breakthrough coach apologized profusely and recommended I try someone else. Even with all the difficulties, after that call, I *knew* this was the program I needed and wanted. But I still didn't enroll. Even though my coach was fantastic and helped me to significantly shift my mindset in just two calls, I doubted my intuition.

How could I possibly spend that kind of money and invest in myself when we were just getting back on our feet after the expensive relocation to Hawai'i? I felt like I would be taking food out of the mouths of my kids. Was I being selfish? At the time, we did not have that kind of disposable income. I talked it over with my husband, and he insisted we didn't have the money. He suggested that I should just go and read some books. This, I knew, was not the mindset that I had just learned, even though currently one does not need certification to become a coach. But for me, being certified was an essential and non-negotiable piece of the equation.

A few weeks later, after stewing with anger and resentment at my husband's unwillingness to support me, I decided to make a call to discuss the program, anyway. A nagging voice insisted that I just call for information. On the other end of the line, the woman was patient with me and answered all of my questions. Honestly, I believe I called because I wanted her to convince me to make the investment. I wanted her to make the decision for me. During that call, she told me something so profound, that it literally changed my decision-making process. Every time she invested in herself, she explained, the Universe repaid the action with whatever it was she needed. This concept revolutionized my thinking. If I shifted into a vibration of abundance, I would attract more abundance. Hanging out with the scarcity mindset crowd was only going to attract more lack.

With no idea of how I would pay off the investment, following that profound discussion with my breakthrough coach and experiencing my own transformation, I finally trusted in myself and made the decision to enroll. And do you know what? That woman was correct. Every single time I have made a decision to invest in myself, the Universe has repaid me in dividends.

Although my husband was initially livid, he began to see positive changes and growth in me. I would talk with him about what I was learning, but many times I felt like he wasn't listening. Then one day a few months later, he came home with a shovel. "I hesitate to tell you this story, but we needed a shovel," he said. "I put the intention out there, and today

I found this shovel lying on the side of the road. You taught me how to manifest what I needed."

During my time in the program, I began manifesting money, cheap airfare, free food, and clothing. Although it didn't directly help me pay off the program, these items alleviated costs elsewhere in the budget. So indirectly, it was still getting paid off. Also, while in the program, I began coaching my own clients. Although it was only a few, and I wasn't charging my value at the time, the Universe showed me that my action was paying off. Finally, just a few weeks after graduating from the program, the Universe made its final payment.

Each year, at the school where I work, teachers have the opportunity to earn extra money in the summer by working on an area to improve or change their respective curricula. I was asked to lead one of these programs, but was told I wouldn't be getting paid since it was just viewed as part of my job. I understood, and honestly, didn't think twice about it at the time. I had literally penned sentence number fifty-five in the 5 x 55 process: "*Thank you, Universe for the money to pay off my coaching program.*" (I will teach you this 5 x 55 process in a future chapter), when I got a call to see my supervisor. They had decided, after talking it through with several other administrators, that I would be paid for leading the teacher workshop, because it really was above and beyond my actual job description. I was asked to sign the agreement, and when I looked at the amount I was being paid, I literally laughed out loud. It was exactly one hundred dollars more than I needed to pay off the program. The Universe not only paid, but paid with interest!

Over these past few years, since graduating and earning my Law of Attraction coaching certificate, I have spent thousands of dollars on myself and my business. I invested in another program to help me launch my online coaching business, I regularly attend workshops and conferences, and I invested in hiring my book coach so I could write this book. So far, I have made back—plus more—on each investment (except perhaps for this book, because as of this writing, it is not yet published). However, I know that in Divine timing, I will make it back, because those were the best decisions to make my dream a reality.

Sometimes we don't make the best decisions. Notice that I did not use the words "wrong" or "incorrect." I don't believe in wrong choices. I think they're just lessons—or redirections. When we made the decision to move to Hawai'i, I began to panic that it was the wrong one. It was my very wise, and much younger friend Lisa, who gave me some of the best advice I have ever gotten. She told me, "Just because you made the decision to move to Hawai'i, doesn't mean you can never make another decision." She was correct. What if moving here had been a disaster? What if we couldn't make it financially, professionally, personally, or socially? The answer is, we could have just made another decision. It truly is that easy!

I work with a coach who will tell you she lit thousands of dollars on fire. Literally, she lost seventy thousand dollars in one transaction! Not all of her investments initially panned out. However, they *eventually* did, because even though she lost money at that moment, she did not stop making decisions or taking action. She didn't give up and allow fear to paralyze her. As a result, she now earns seven-figures as a coach.

Inspired Assignment
Fear delays decision making. When you allow your ego to speak louder than your intuition, you not only distrust yourself, but also the Universe. The Universe doesn't respond to indecision. It doesn't acknowledge ambiguity. It responds to action. Using these steps, you will learn to make decisions quickly, accelerating the manifestation process.

1. Listen to your intuition: You have the answer; it lives inside of you. Too many people believe they have to go to an external source for an answer. They begin asking family and friends for their opinions. The problem with that is most of them will probably discourage you from investing in yourself. Not because they are trying to be malicious, but because unenlightened people operate from fear (ego), so they believe they are trying to protect you. When you need to make a decision, ask yourself, "Should I..." (fill in the blank). Whatever answer comes to you in five seconds, is the answer. If nothing comes to you, quiet your mind with meditation (you can find several good meditations on *YouTube*). Ask the Universe for a

specific sign if you need confirmation. But the bottom line is, *trust* yourself! I recently had to make a decision and used this process. Immediately, the answer was yes. I went to my Angels Answer oracle card deck and asked for confirmation. I shuffled the cards, laid them out, and pulled my answer. I almost fell over. I chose the "Yes" card from forty-four cards! I'm not sure there could be any more apparent sign.

2. For some, step one will still be difficult, and you will need lots of practice before it becomes second nature like it has for me. If this is the case for you, make a list of pros and cons, but try not to analyze or judge as you write these. Simply record the first things that come to you. Once the list is finished, go back and determine which ones are fear-based and cross them off the list. Your ego has no place here.

Example: *Should I invest in the coaching program?*

Pros
- Certification upon graduation
- Live classes with a teacher
- Replays of each class
- Put in a pod to work with others
- Can coach during the program and begin making money
- Opportunity to positively impact many people's lives
- 1:1 feedback and assessments
- AM classes do not interfere with my work schedule

Cons
- PM classes are during work hours
- May not make back money
- Ten-month commitment

3. Make a decision: Even if the decision is no, make it and move on. If it is yes, and most times it will be, take *action*. Remember, the Universe speaks frequency. To get on the same frequency, your vibration must match. The action raises your vibration,

aligning to the frequency of your desire. I wanted to be a Law of Attraction coach. Once I made a decision and enrolled, I shifted my belief, which changed my vibration, which aligned me with the perfect program.

I learned another vital phrase in Mrs. Naffin's Latin class: *Carpe Diem*! According to <u>Merriam-Webster dictionary</u> it is simply defined as the enjoyment of the pleasures of the moment without concern for the future:

> *This Latin phrase, which literally means "pluck the day," was used by the Roman poet Horace to express the idea that we should enjoy life while we can. His full injunction, "carpe diem quam minimum credula postero," can be translated as "pluck the day, trusting as little as possible in the next one," but carpe diem alone has come to be used as shorthand for this entire idea, which is more widely known as "seize the day."*

I love this definition, because it alludes to the most important and most challenging step when manifesting: don't be concerned about the future; focus on the present. Remember, it cannot be overstated: the *how* is *none of your damn business*!

You know the phrase: when in Rome, do as the Romans. Make a decision! *Carpe Diem*!

CHAPTER 8

"L" is for Listen

We have two ears and one mouth so we can listen twice as much as we speak. ~ Epictetus, *(Greek philosopher, AD 55-135)*

Step Two: **"L" is for Listen.** Years ago, when I was interviewing for my very first teaching job, a principal asked me, "Is there a difference between hearing and listening?" I answered yes, and responded with an apparently surprising answer, because the principal threw down his pen and told me that it was a profound answer, especially since I was only twenty-two years old, and hadn't professionally taught one day in a classroom. I'm sorry to admit that I don't know what the heck I said, I just remember that I answered something about listening being way more important than hearing.

Here's how *"listening"* is defined in the Merriam Webster dictionary:

Definition of *listen*

transitive verb
archaic : to give ear to : hear

intransitive verb
1: to pay attention to sound *listen* to music

2: to hear something with thoughtful attention **:** give consideration *listen* to a plea

3: to be alert to catch an expected sound *listen* for his step

Although the traditional definition of listening applies to this chapter, listening goes beyond your ears. To manifest your heart's desires, you need to listen with your eyes, heart, mind, and gut.

Every day we are bombarded with thousands of messages, many of which we ignore. We seek these answers outside of ourselves, but the truth is, every answer lies within us. Many people seek out psychics, mediums, and coaches like me to help them discover these answers. There is no answer "out there." You have them all *inside*. The problem we have, as humans, is that we ignore our own intuition daily, and we refuse to listen to what we know intrinsically. Trusting yourself is the key to unlocking your heart's desires.

You need to listen to signs that the Universe whispers, whether it be in a number you see over and over again, a feather on the ground, a heart in a rock, or...fill in the blank. This is the way the Universe is trying to get you to listen, but you have allowed fear to disconnect you from the powerful voice that beckons so loudly and clearly, that you may as well be deaf. Actually, the deaf probably hear the best because they are so much more sensitive to vibration, which is the Universe's first language.

Many people have experienced, or have at least heard of, mother's intuition. I'm a mom, and I'm telling you it is a real thing. I knew the moment my oldest had strep throat, or my youngest had an ear infection. I knew when they were up to no good (quiet is always a bad sign with toddlers). I never once questioned my knowing—and by the way, I was always right. So, why did I trust my gut for my children, but I didn't listen to it for myself?

As I was writing this chapter to teach this step, I had to laugh at the synchronicity the Universe showed me to confirm I was on the right path. Not going to lie, I was watching the reality TV show, *The Bachelorette,* when I got confirmation.

Hannah, the Bachelorette, was down to two guys. The next step was to introduce them both to her parents. The first guy's visit progressed easily and effortlessly; the family loved him. They laughed and smiled the entire day. Their date was fun, romantic, and joyful, and they left each other wanting more. The next day, however, guy number two walked through the door, and immediately there was a difference. You could see it in how the family looked at him; you could hear it in the tone of their voices as they spoke to him and asked questions. You could feel it in your own heart that they were not connecting with him in the same way as they did with guy number one. When the couple headed out on their date in a boat, Hannah became seasick, and their conversation was serious and strained. She admitted that she didn't know what she was feeling, and expressed her doubts. They both cried a lot and the date ended awkwardly.

As an observer, I could not believe that she was ignoring the obvious visible signs the Universe was using to get her attention. I was screaming at the TV, "He's clearly not the one!" Hannah was so caught up in making the wrong decision, that she wasn't listening to her heart, her gut, and how she was feeling...or the freaking signs the Universe was using to basically hit her over the head! Guess what? Spoiler alert. I was right. Hannah chose guy number two, and they broke up!

I learned how valuable it is to listen when I was trying to manifest my dream job in Hawai'i. You'll actually read how I manifested this dream life in a subsequent chapter, but I need to go backward first. I had interviewed to serve as one of the Co-Directors of Student Activities, and was awaiting the news. It would take a few weeks to make a decision, they told me, but I'm not very patient. Deep down I *knew* the job was mine, yet I refused to listen to my intuition. Fear held me captive in its vice, causing me to distrust my gut. During my lunch break, I decided to listen to an abundance coach named Christie Marie Sheldon, whose expertise is removing abundance blocks. Serendipitously, the topic was on asking the Universe to reveal a sign, so you know you are on the right path. I remember looking at the clock; it was a little after twelve noon, and I asked aloud, "Universe, I need a crystal clear sign that this job is mine."

A few hours later, I left work to attend my first meeting for the Hawai'i Association of Middle-Level educators. The meeting was at a private school just a few miles away. Now, understand something. This school (like mine) was on a campus, not simply one building like most schools on the mainland. It was huge. There were many different buildings and areas around the campus, and I had no idea where this meeting was located precisely. A helpful security officer directed me to the main office to check-in, but the secretary insisted on walking me to the meeting because, she said, "you will never find it on your own." She was right! We finally arrived at the door and she said, "Here you go."

I looked at the sign on the door, and it read: Student Activities Office. I could barely get out the next sentence. I asked, "This is the student activities office?" She must have thought I couldn't read and said, "Yes. You seem so surprised." She had no idea why I was startled, nor could she know that I was *freaking out* inside. *This was the sign!* Of all the buildings where this meeting could have taken place, it was held in the office of my future job!

Really, let this sink in a second. That meeting could have been *anywhere*, but here it was in the parallel office I would soon occupy at my own school! If that wasn't enough, the first person I met in that meeting was the Director of Student Activities at the school. I couldn't *freaking* believe it. I don't know what sign could have been any clearer! And yes, I got the job a few weeks later!

We have two ears and one mouth for a reason. I continue to learn this lesson every day. It's not that I talk a lot, or because I think I am so wise and have so much to say. It's actually how I once believed I processed information. I learned, however, that listening actually helps me process faster. I was told by two psychics that one of my spiritual lessons of this lifetime is to learn to listen and trust myself. I can be very indecisive. Listening has allowed me to connect with my higher self and to truly trust my gut. I make decisions quickly and confidently now. By trusting myself first, it is easier to relax and believe that the Universe is working behind the scenes for my highest good.

Inspired Assignment
You will never learn to truly listen to yourself or the Universe if you don't quiet your mind. I am an Aries and a Type A personality, which is strong and outspoken, but I worry a lot and can stress easily. My husband would tell me to "shut off my brain" because I am thinking and processing 24/7. Meditation, I have discovered, is the fastest vehicle for learning to hear myself.

Meditation is free and it's easier to do than you might think. You don't need to become a Buddhist monk and meditate for hours a day to achieve Zen results. To begin, you need five minutes and a quiet place. I like to meditate in the morning, but any time of day is fine. Find a quiet place. You can sit, lie down, just get comfortable. If you fall asleep, that's ok. You can use guided meditation, music, or just sit in absolute quiet. It doesn't matter; you can't do it incorrectly.

In the beginning of my meditation practice, I attended a fifteen-minute morning meditation. A chime signaled when it was time to begin and end, and we would sit together in absolute silence. For days, at first my brain would wander, thinking about the papers I needed to grade, the lesson I was about to deliver that day, what I needed to make for dinner... Fifteen minutes felt like an eternity!

Then instinctively, as a thought would come, I learned to just acknowledge it and allow it to pass. Instead of dwelling on those thoughts, I focused on my breath, noticing it go in and out. Then I would envision a hot air balloon. I would put my thoughts in the basket and watch it float away. Eventually, I sat in silence and connected to my breath for fifteen to twenty minutes.

It is ideal if you can meditate daily, but doing it whenever you can is still beneficial. Now, I use a combination of methods. I use the *Calm* app, *YouTube* meditations, and silence. There is also a *Stop, Breathe & Think Kids* app, which we have used with our students. Try using it to meditate as a family.

Mediation is a practice. It should become part of your daily routine. Allow yourself to tap in to your intuitive power. The quieter you become, the more signs the Universe will whisper to you. Are you listening?

CHAPTER 9

Signs, Signs, Everywhere There's Signs

Synchronicity is God sending us messages anonymously. ~ Deepak Chopra

I had just fallen back to sleep. My daughters had landed safely at JFK airport and were heading to baggage claim to meet grandma and grandpa for their ten-day visit in Pennsylvania. Suddenly, my phone rang and my heart stopped to see a Facetime call coming in from my oldest. She had texted just forty-five minutes ago to let me know they landed and that all was well. What could have happened in that time? Why was she Facetiming and not just texting or calling?! I answered the call in the dark, with my one eye barely open, to find my best male friend—my brother from another mother—greeting me. My daughters had bumped into Uncle Jer, with his wife and kids, while Jer was checking the boards for his flight status.

What would be the chances? This was not planned. I'd had no idea they were going on vacation. He had no idea of the exact dates of the girls' visit to the mainland. We had just stayed with them in March and talked about possibly seeing them again in the summer. And here they were, among thousands of travelers, at the exact same place and time!

Swiss psychiatrist, Carl Jung, coined the term synchronicity: "a concept which holds that events are 'meaningful coincidences' if they occur with no causal relationship, yet seem to be meaningfully related" ...blah, blah, blah. What the heck does that even mean? To me, a synchronicity is a God nod, or God wink. Synchronicities are coincidences with a message.

Every day we are bombarded with texts, emails, social media notifications, and phone calls. While technology keeps us connected, it has disconnected us from the Universe's direct line. Every day we dismiss messages that appear to us in the tangible form of feathers, number sequences, people, and billboards with literal messages, all screaming for our attention. By bringing our attention to these signs, we can manifest our desires so much faster. Synchronicities are signs that we are on the right path.

You're probably wondering, "But Kelly, how do I know which signs are from the Universe and which ones are just a billboard advertising underwear?" You'll know they are messages for you when they start showing up every day and consistently. One synchronicity that many of my clients report seeing is the number 1111. They will look at the clock at 11:11 a.m. or p.m. They will see a car with the license plate 1111. Others will see sequences of numbers like 555, 888, 333, 222.

Some people see numbers that are significant to them. A friend of mine was seeing her childhood home address consistently. She knows I love this stuff, so she reached out to me. First of all, I was so proud of her that she even noticed the Universe was trying to get her attention. Most people would blow it off. My "woo woo-ness" had finally rubbed off on her, and she knew this had to be a message. Together, we looked it up on my favorite site where I check angel numbers, and she was astounded when she read what the numbers meant; it was exactly the message she needed at that moment. Since her desire has manifested, she no longer sees those numbers. Rest assured, the Universe didn't give up on her. It still sends her signs as she needs them, but in other ways.

In 2011, on our second trip to Hawai'i, I knew I wanted to move here. I began the manifestation process that I teach in this book. Through my own spiritual awakening, and learning about the Law of Attraction, I knew

I should ask for signs that this was the next chapter of my life. Two years later, in 2013, I manifested a two-week internship at a prestigious private school in Honolulu. That was it. My entire focus became teaching and moving to the islands.

During that time, I would see the number 808 every day: morning and night. For the uninitiated, 808 is the area code for Hawai'i. I would literally screech in delight every time I saw it. I started taking screenshots as proof! My husband really thought I was losing it. But then, he and the kids started noticing it on their own, too!

This went on for months. Literally, every single day, morning and evening, I would inevitably look at my phone, or the clock, at precisely 8:08. I am really not sure how I came across it, or who introduced me to the sacred angel number website, but when I checked the message there, I almost fell over. For those new to numerology, eight is the number of wealth and abundance. Turned on its side, it is the infinity symbol! My dream of moving to Hawai'i was becoming a quick reality.

Numbers were not the only sign I received. I had now trained my awareness to be open to the Universe's private line and was dialed in. Soon, it seemed that everywhere I went, there was some Hawaiian connection. I recall walking into *Bath and Body Works* at our local mall in Pennsylvania, and being drawn to a display of lotions. It was the Hawaiian collection. Our next stop was the Disney Store, and right as we walked in, there was the Hawaiian doll from the *It's a Small World* ride. Another day, we walked into the dollar store and there was a vast luau display. I looked at my daughters and said, "Pack your bags, we are moving to Hawai'i!"

The signs kept coming. We would watch a movie, and low and behold, there were Hawaiian references. I'd turn on the TV just as Hawai'i, *5-0* was starting with its catchy theme song; we honestly had never even watched that show. One night, while we were out for an ice cream treat, I looked down at a display, and there was a cake with a lei on it, that read *Aloha*. People, this was Pennsylvania, not California or Florida, where maybe you'd see an island reference. This was eastern PA! There were so many other signs that I could probably write a whole book on synchronicities!

And here's the craziest thing. As soon as we landed in Hawai'i, I stopped seeing 8:08 everywhere. In fact, as I was typing this chapter, I looked at my phone at 8:08! I gave myself chills, or chicken skin, as they call it here! It was confirmation that this was the story I needed to write!

Imagine ignoring all of those signs. You probably think that's impossible, but I'm telling you, I have coaching clients every day who are not tuned in. They miss the messages, because they dismiss it as merely coincidence.

Have you ever heard the story of Christopher Columbus? Apparently, Christopher Columbus discovered the moon, because everyone else was too busy looking down at the ground to find gold. One day, Christopher Columbus had a sore neck, and he looked up. Holy smokers! There was the moon. Obviously, this is not a true story, and I don't know who wrote it. The point is, stop looking down for the gold, and start looking up for the signs that the Universe is shining onto you. Or, as my wise psychic, George, told me at my last reading, "Get your head out of your ass!"

Now that you realize you have the power to tap in, you can confirm whether the desire you want to manifest is for your highest good. Let's say, for example, that there's a job you really want. Ask the Universe to show you signs that this job is the perfect match for you. If it is, you may start seeing numbers of the future address of the company, or you may meet someone who works there or knows someone who works there. You may hear an ad for the company on the radio, or notice a sign you've never seen before. If you don't get any messages like this, take it as a sign to move on. Something better is coming.

When you begin seeing the signs, you realize your manifestation is on the way in divine timing. You can relax and detach from the outcome, and the dreaded "how" your desire will manifest. You can be like, "Cool, it's on its way; I got confirmation."

Inspired assignment

You will learn to ask the Universe for a sign or message, but as you will read in a future chapter, the Universe doesn't have a day planner. It's not that you will get that message this afternoon, it could take a while. Simply be aware. Practice patience. Practice watching for the signs using this process:

1. Dial into awareness: Identify an object or number you want to see in your life. Choose something you don't usually notice. Tell the Universe, "Universe, for the next week or so, show me (object). Thank you!" Over the course of the next week, pay attention to how many times you see that object. Snap a picture of it, or try to document it somehow to keep a reference.

2. Accept the Call: Now, focus on a desire you want to manifest. Ask the Universe to show you signs that this manifestation is for your highest good and that you are on the right path. By accepting this call, stop looking for the gold, and look for the moon. You will get your answer in divine timing, so if you're put on hold, know it's because it's really the next call you should answer.

3. Hang Up: If the line seems dead or busy, do *not* freak out. If the Universe isn't answering, you need to believe that this is not for your highest good. Thank the Universe for having your back. Simply hang up and call again with another desire. Repeat this process anytime you need confirmation.

The Universe's calling system is far better than any phone you will ever own. It will text you, call you, leave messages, even if you put it in airplane mode or silence it. It rings 24/7, three hundred and sixty-five days of the year, whether you answer or not. The Universe's battery life is infinite and won't die on you. Check your dang voicemail; there's a message waiting just for you!

CHAPTER 10

"O" is for Open

A mind is like a parachute. It doesn't work if it is not open. ~ Frank Zappa

Knock knock. Who's there? Opportunity. Opportunity who? Slams door. Yep, I wish this were just one of those knock-knock jokes, but for so many of my clients, it's no joke. They often close the door when an opportunity comes knocking because they think the knocking was not meant for them. The closed sign is in the window and they are not open for business.

The third step in my manifestation process is "O" for Open; you need to be open to opportunities and new ideas. The Universe may give you something that is actually better than what you expected or were looking for. Being open means opening your heart, mind, eyes, and ears to what is possible, not merely what you *think* you want. Of course, you can't just sit around waiting for the Universe to drop it in your lap, like the Amazon drone delivering a package. Action is still required on your part. That action could be simply researching or investigating the possibilities. *How* they come to you is none of your business. More about that later.

"Now, Kelly," I hear you thinking. "What you just wrote totally contradicted your first step of the process: Ask. In that chapter, you told me to get crystal clear on my desire because the Universe doesn't like ambiguity."

Yes! You are correct, and I wish I could reach out and give you a gold star for being an attentive reader. Let me explain.

While it is essential for you to be clear on your desire, remember, the Universe is actually responding to your vibration. By asking you to get clear and focus on the details, I actually tricked you. Sorry. Not sorry. (It's like when I try to sneak veggies into my kids' smoothies; it's for good intentions.) By asking you to get clear and write out every detail, I got you excited about the manifestation. This elevates your vibration, aligning you to attract your desire. However, sometimes the Universe delivers something way better than you could have imagined, so you need to be open to other possibilities.

My oldest daughter had gotten her driver's permit. Unlike most parents, my husband and I were thrilled that we would have another driver in the family. We made the decision to begin looking for a car. Of course, she had a clear idea on the car she wanted—doesn't every sixteen-year-old who is about to drive? A Tesla was out of the question for many reasons, so she decided she wanted a Toyota Corolla or a Rav 4. We weren't in any big hurry, after all, she had just gotten her permit; however, we wanted the car sooner than later, so that she could practice driving in it for the road test.

Being her mama and a manifesting Goddess, I set this intention at the next new moon, and let it go. Or so I thought. A few weeks later, I remembered that one of our colleagues was moving off the island and he had a Rav 4. *Perfect!* Immediately, I sent him an email asking if it was available and how much he wanted for it. To my dismay, he replied that it was already sold. I was actually furious. Here was the perfect car, and it was *gone*. I cursed the Universe. How could you let me miss this opportunity? This was the perfect car. It was the model we wanted, it had low mileage, the color was exactly what our daughter wanted, and we knew the owner and the car's history. *It was perfect!* Or so we thought...

A week later, a colleague stopped my husband at work. He heard that we were looking for a car and offered to give us his Subaru Legacy for *free*. My husband laughed and blew him off, thinking it was a joke. If you knew these two, you'd totally understand. Our friend was serious, but there was a catch. The car had been in an accident and had body damage on the driver's side. Because of the accident, he wasn't sure if the vehicle had mechanical issues and he couldn't verify how safe it was. However, the car only had forty-five thousand miles on it, and the inside was pristine. After looking at it and assessing the damage, our mechanic determined it was safe. It needed an alignment, new tires, and a few minor items that weren't even related to the accident. When all was said and done, the car cost a mere three hundred dollars. Since our friend refused to take any money, insisting that the car was no longer being driven and was just costing him money sitting on the street, we gave him a gift card as a small token of our sincere appreciation. Energy exchange is vital in the manifestation process, and money is simply energy.

Holy moly, I had freaking manifested a car! It proved to be the perfect first vehicle for a sixteen-year-old driver. She wouldn't feel as bad if she scraped a wall—which is entirely possible in Hawai'i, as the parking spots are ridiculously small compared to the mainland. My daughter passed her driving test on the first try, and we all have "Jerb" to thank. (That's what she named her car.) Initially, my daughter wasn't wholly sold (pun intended) on this car. While she thought she wanted a Corolla or a Rav 4, those weren't the cars for her. Instead, this car allowed us (her parents) to cover more of the budget and put less of a cash drain on her. She still has to pay for gas and minor upkeep, but in the long run, that Rav 4 would have cost her most of her savings and would have required her to get a job.

Actually, the Subaru is one of the best cars we have ever had. It's everything we wanted and more. And it was *free*! Because we were open to expanded opportunities, we got a better car than the Rav 4 I thought we "missed." The experience taught my daughter (and reminded me) to stay open to whatever comes through when you are trying to manifest. If we hadn't been open to another type of car, we would have never gotten Jerb. The Universe has the power to turn our disappointment into delight.

Inspired Assignment

So, how can you learn to open your mind, heart, and eyes to infinite possibilities? Here are three ways to open yourself to opportunities:

1. In a journal, begin to write out everything you want to manifest. I like to write my intentions during the new moon. The New Moon

is the best time to set intentions to manifest your desires. Use the full moon energy when you need to release emotions and events that no longer serve you. After each one, write the words, "this or better." This phraseology indicates to the Universe that you are open to accepting this or better, if that is what the Universe determines is right for you.

Example:
- *Ten or more paid-in-full clients...this or better*
- *$5,000.00 to pay off credit card debt...this or better*

2. Keep your eyes, ears, mind, and heart open. While you see potentially only one outcome, the Universe has an infinite supply. Don't just sit around and wait for your manifestation to come to fruition. Be active; look around and observe. Pursue and investigate.

3. Envision your manifestation coming to you in different ways. Don't be confused, however! This does not mean that you should try to manipulate the outcome, as I did with the Rav 4. Sometimes, you can reach the same destination by car, bus, or train. Let the Universe decide if the way you envision is the fastest and best method of transportation.

Doors have two primary functions. They open and they close. When doors are open, we can see the interior of the whole room. When they are closed, we merely see a steel or wooden frame, preventing us from entering. Which door are you? Closed and locked out of all that awaits on the other side? Or open to the Universe's infinite spacious home?

CHAPTER 11

Fear

Everything you want is on the other side of fear. ~ Jack Canfield

People say I am brave because I moved my family halfway around the world to Hawai'i. I'm not brave. Patients battling cancer are brave. The men and women on the front lines fighting for our freedom are brave. The 9/11 responders are brave. I do believe I have something in common with these groups of people, however. We allowed our faith to be bigger than our fear.

You've probably seen the many "definitions" of fear on Pinterest or social media. One definition I especially resonate with is *"false evidence appearing real."* Many times, we are not actually afraid of what we think we are; it's the unknown outcome that we are afraid of. Indeed, is there any evidence to support our fear? Probably not. Fear is self-created. We are not born with it; we learn it. Therefore, we can unlearn it.

Babies are a good example. How many times have you heard a parent say, "my child has no fear"? If a toddler sees a body of water, it doesn't sense danger. Instead, the child will happily run towards it. When our oldest daughter was little, she loved to play in our small above ground pool. One day she was playing, and the next moment, she sank to the bottom and just sat there. Of course, my husband and I freaked out and immediately brought her to the surface. In her mind, there was nothing to fear. But our reaction stunned her, and as she searched our panic faces, she began to wail. Could the consequence have been deadly? Absolutely! Children die each year due to drowning, and by no means am I downplaying that. But the point is, we need to return to the child who walks through his fears confidently. Because the only way *out* is *through*.

Our fear is not in the tangible or intangible outcome; it is in trusting the unknown. We waste our time and energy creating worst-case scenarios when they seldom ever happen. Even if something terrible happens, there's always a blessing in disguise or a silver lining (more on that later). Instead of focusing on success, our fears have already created failure.

Are you aware that you have a first responder? Are you plugged into the protective power of the Universe? Your faith is your shield, your weapon, and your ability to combat any fear. The Universe's line of defense is more significant than any army here on Earth. There's no reason to be afraid.

I wish I could go back and tell myself that in 2014 when we decided to move to Oahu. I was terrified. What if we couldn't find a place to live? What if my husband started his business again, and it failed? What if the kids hated their new school and couldn't make friends? How would we survive without our friends and family nearby? There were a million reasons to be afraid, and a million reasons we should just stay in Pennsylvania, our home state. I was teaching in a high achieving school district and was at the peak of my career. My husband's business was thriving, with over twelve hundred clients. My daughters loved their school. We had a beautiful home in a safe community. My in-laws lived only a mile away, and my family was within driving distance. We had a perfect life, but I had a dream. I wasn't going to let fear steal it.

We were moving to a place where we knew no one; we didn't have any family nearby. My husband had only moved a mile from his childhood home. At the most, I had moved a whopping thirty miles. Sure, we had visited Hawai'i twice, but we really didn't understand or appreciate the significant cultural nuances. Like most ignorant mainlanders, we were lured by the white sandy beaches, gorgeous sunsets, and consistent warm temperatures. But the reality of any change or relocation, is that there is a steep learning curve—one that I didn't anticipate and was completely naive about.

I'm not exaggerating; the first six months were pretty much hell. Just because you move to paradise, doesn't mean that your life automatically becomes paradise. Within the first few weeks, I was convinced this was the biggest mistake I had ever made, and it felt like it was all my fault. I accepted all of the blame and guilt, and allowed the monster of fear to keep me gripped in its vice, and awake most nights. I lost all faith in the Universe and myself, and I waited for the fear monster to swallow me whole.

Guess what? I'm still here, alive and kicking. None of the dire stories my family or I created came true. What changed? I changed. I remembered that the same Universe that helped me make this dream a reality, was the same Universe that could rescue me. At that moment, I decided. That's it. I simply decided that my faith was bigger than my fear.

And guess what else? The Universe swooped in and rescued me. Within only two weeks, my husband got a small promotion. My colleagues quickly became friends, and within a few months, we had met families who became our 'Ohana (family). My girls started to love their new school and made awesome friends. In fact, my youngest had a busier social life than the rest of the three of us combined. Six months later, we were able to move from the apartment my kids hated and we celebrated Christmas in our newly purchased condo!

Now, here we are almost a decade later. My husband earned a huge promotion and loves his job. My daughters are not only thriving academically, but socially, personally, and emotionally. They have so many educational opportunities that they just wouldn't have had in public school. Our friendships and relationships with colleagues are like none we've ever experienced. I left the classroom to work my dream job, earned my coaching and reiki certifications, and am writing this book. I found a spiritual community that supports my transformation and growth unconditionally. I allowed my faith to become bigger than my fear, and all of my dreams are coming true.

It is my belief that we are born with lessons to learn in this lifetime. One of my biggest lessons is trusting myself and the decisions I make. I have no doubt that combatting my fear was just another lesson I needed to learn.

When shit hit the fan, my first thought was to move back to Pennsylvania. Recede to the place I knew: return to the familiar. It's like when we are sick, and we reach for the blanket or the bowl of soup that will bring us comfort. It will bring some relief for a short time, but then we are right back to where we began. Back to the same patterns that got us nowhere.

Inspired Assignment

How do you begin to overcome fear? How do you make a change to get you out of your comfort zone? First, name a fear that you need to face. Start small; don't try to conquer your worst fear. Identify one action step you can take each day.

For example, my oldest daughter was terrified of riding the public bus here in Hawai'i. She was afraid she would get on and off at the incorrect stop and that she would become lost. I remember thinking, "Okay, kid, not trying to downplay your fears, but this is an island, so how lost can you possibly get?" To help conquer her fear, I rode the bus with her a few times. Once she was comfortable, she rode one stop by herself and I was there to meet her. That's all it took. Now she and her friends ride all over the island with no issue. Sure, they have gotten on or off at the wrong stop, but it was no problem. She realized the worst-case scenario was actually not a big deal. She simply checked the schedule and got back on the correct bus.

Are you like me at restaurants? I always order the same thing when I go to certain places. Why should I order something new and take the chance of not enjoying it—especially here in Hawai'i, where food is super expensive? The reason is because I need to learn to live outside of my comfort zone. If I don't enjoy it, the worst-case scenario is that I spent money on something I hated. I didn't die. No one got hurt. Best-case scenario: I just ate one of the best new dishes in my life! I challenge you to try something new each day: a food, a product or a drink. You never know, it could soon become your new favorite.

I can hear you again, "Kelly, come on. Riding a bus and trying new foods pale in comparison to the fears holding me hostage. How is this going to help me?"

Each time you overcome one small fear, your confidence will grow. As your confidence grows, you will start to identify broader fears and be able to face them faster and courageously. Those people whom you've envied from afar or looked up to for their bravery, yep, that is you—the *new you.*

Not everyone wants to move, not even to Hawai'i. But all of us have fears that are holding us back from living the life we long to live. Some fears could feel huge, but when you break them down, they may actually be easier to manage than you think. "Do one thing every day that scares you." If you follow this advice for a month, you will have overcome thirty new things. If you do it for the year: three hundred and sixty-five fears overcome! Do you even have that many fears to face?

Looking back, the Universe always took care of me. I have had everything I needed and more. In the midst of my fears about our move, I realized, why wouldn't the Universe take care of me now? Just because I moved six thousand miles away, didn't mean I could no longer tap in to it. The Universe is omnipotent and omnipresent. Everything always works out for our highest good if we just surrender our fears.

CHAPTER 12

"H" is for How

The how is none of your damn business. ~ Kelly Weaver

Every year we host a variety show at my school. Any student from grades seven to twelve is encouraged to audition. Over the years, my organizing partner and I have seen some pretty exciting acts. These are kids, so to be fair—I know they tried, but man—some of those acts would make Simon Cowell launch into a scathing tirade. But then there was one. That one kid who should be on the next episode of America's Got Talent.

When she walked into the audition, I'm not going to lie, I wasn't expecting very much. She was an unassuming seventh grader here to show us a magic trick using cards. Then she stepped up to the microphone, and the voice that spoke was an articulate and wise old soul, like she had been there, done that before. What happened in the next five minutes was genuinely magical (pun intended). As she exited the audition, my partner and I looked at each other in complete disbelief at what just happened.

Unfortunately, while her act was outstanding, it wouldn't work in a gym of fourteen hundred students. There was no way the entire audience could see the cards like we could in this intimate setting. After we explained this to her, she decided to do a different trick involving several rings that interlocked. For four minutes, the audience was utterly captivated by this seventh-grader's ring trick. As her act came to an end, the audience erupted into a standing ovation. The cheering students were losing their minds!

For the next show, she decided to up the ante. She rolled out a big box on the stage and commanded her assistant (a fellow student) to get in. He pretended to be reluctant because he knew what was about to go down. As the background music played, she sharpened several knives on the box. While he screamed and pounded on the box, desperately trying to get out, she jammed sword after sword into the box until there was silence.

Now let me tell you something. I have been in education for over twenty years, and until this point, I have never witnessed a moment where every single person, student and staff alike, was wholly engaged and on the edge of their seat. When she opened the box, and her assistant was gone, the crowd went absolutely nuts. She then removed each sword, spun the box around in the precise timing of the music, and opened the door again. This time, her assistant sat there seemingly terrified, and jumped out unscathed. Throughout the pandemonium of screams, you could hear the same question being asked over and over again. *How* did she do that?!

As the audience regained composure, and the students were dismissed, many of them came to inspect the box and begged her to tell them how she had done this trick? Any good magician will never tell you his or her methods because knowing *how* ruins the magic of the performance.

Step Four in the manifestation process: "H" is for How. How your desires manifest is none of your damn business. Sorry. Not sorry. It is not up to you to try to orchestrate the outcome. While you may think you know how your desire will come to fruition, the Universe has a million other tricks up its sleeve that you can't, and haven't, even imagined.

Many people believe that by letting go of the outcome they are giving up. Surrender is not giving up; surrender is allowing yourself to receive. It's aligning your vibration to the same frequency of the desire. Remember from the previous chapter: the Universe doesn't speak a language. It speaks vibration. If you are worried about *how* you desire will manifest, you will only attract more worry and doubt. You must trust and believe that your desire is coming. Don't ruin the magic by trying to manipulate how it will arrive.

My oldest daughter frequently performs in her school's plays and musicals. When she was fourteen, she and several other students were invited by the performing arts department to perform at the Fringe Festival in Edinburgh, Scotland. Each year, thousands of thespians gather at the festival to showcase their talents. All ages and levels of expertise are represented. It was indeed a once in a lifetime opportunity for her, but there was one big problem, uh, I mean opportunity. I didn't have that kind of money to pay for the cost of the trip. Also, there was no way I was allowing a fourteen-year-old girl to travel halfway around the world without my husband or me going with her. So, now we were looking at an incredibly expensive trip. *How* was I going to pay for that?

My husband didn't even want to attend the information meeting because he was adamant that there was no way, come hell or high water, that we could afford this. Now, he should know—being married to a manifesting master—this was not a response I could accept. I told him we needed to go to the meeting to gather all of the information, and then we could make a decision. During the meeting, we learned that there would be extensive fundraising as well as other ways that may cut down the cost significantly. He heard "may cut down" the price; I heard "cut cost." We also learned that our cost was not as high as we initially believed, because adults attending had the option of not doing a lot of the activities that were mandatory for students. Because of this, we could use airline miles for me to travel to New York, and I didn't need accommodations there because I could stay with my friends and family on the east coast. Basically, I could build my own package, so there was room for considerable savings.

Armed with this intel, I set the intention that my daughter and I would go to Scotland, while my husband insisted there was no way we could afford this. I had no idea *how* we would do it, but the Universe has shown me over and over again that somehow it would work out. Two weeks later, it revealed it's magic.

My husband was asked to meet with his boss. He didn't know the purpose of the meeting; he just assumed she wanted to touch base about the robotics program he was helping to lead. It was. However, she started by apologizing and informed him that, because the program was considered extracurricular, he should have been receiving a stipend for his time and efforts. All coaches receive extra compensation, since it is outside of their regular job expectations. She told him the amount he would be receiving. It was enough to cover most of the trip expenses, not just for my daughter but for me as well!

As the year progressed, there were a lot of fundraising opportunities. Any money made was divided among all of the students attending. The proceeds from our annual fair, which is used to fund student travel, was also awarded to each of the theatre students. After booking my own flights, and customizing my trip, the stipend my husband received covered the entire remaining cost of our trip.

We had no idea how that money would show up. Even if I had written a list of all the places, ways, and people we could scrounge from, I could never have imagined it would come in the form of a stipend from robotics.

When we landed in Scotland, I looked around at thirty very excited teenagers, one of them my daughter. I smiled and even chuckled, thanking the Universe for this incredible opportunity. Those next ten days of watching my daughter perform on an international stage, driving through rolling green hills and picturesque landscapes, and immersing myself into our own heritage, were life-changing for my daughter and me. When she graduates, we plan to go again, except this time my husband and youngest daughter will be joining us, and we will also travel to Ireland and London. How will we afford it? Hell, if I know. That's none of my damn business! I'll let the Universe work its magic once again.

If I could teach you only one step of the manifestation process, this would be the one. In my humble opinion and experience, it is the most critical step. It is also the most difficult to master. Frankly, there are still times when a desire is not manifesting to my liking and on my timeline, so I try to manipulate the outcome. Each time, I am pleasantly thwarted.

Learning to let go has not only affected how quickly I can manifest, but it has profoundly changed my life in other ways, too. It has taught me to trust not only in a higher power, but in myself. For a long time, I didn't trust any decision I made, which made me live a lot of life in fear and uncertainty. Now, I can make a decision much more quickly and believe that the outcome will always be for my highest good, even when it seems like it's not the one I wanted.

Because I can let go and step back, I have manifested so many positive things into my life. I simply need to ask and trust that all will come to me in perfect timing, The Universe is unfolding exactly as it should.

Inspired Assignment

Learning to let go of *how* is a critical step in the manifestation process. Although it may be a rather abstract concept, let's use an analogy that most have experienced. When you go to a restaurant, the server takes your order and you probably go back to talking with those at the table. You trust that the food will come out the way you desire. You don't leave the restaurant and head to the convenience store to grab a meal in the interim. If the kitchen is short-staffed, or the restaurant is bustling, it may take longer for your meal to come out, but you never doubt that it will be delivered to you. This is the same level of trust and patience you need to have with the Universe.

For this assignment, you will need the guest check template on the page following this assignment, a piece of paper or notebook, a pen, and a small box or container.

1. Place your order. Using the Guest check below, fill in one desire you currently want to manifest within the next thirty days. Remember to ask for what you want in detail, but be open to something better coming along; remember *this or better*! You may have more than one desire you wish to manifest. If that's the case, list each request on a separate guest check. Fold this up and place it in a container. Place the container somewhere out of sight, but somewhere you will remember.

2. Using the notebook or paper, write down every possible way you feel your manifestation may come to fruition. Place it in the container as well.

3. Set a reminder on your phone for thirty days later. On day thirty, open the container and read whether or not your desires have manifested. If so, take out the list of "hows" and see if you predicted the way your manifestation came into being.

If your manifestation did not materialize, do *not* freak out. Remember, if it is meant for your highest good, it may be delayed, but it will arrive in divine timing. Put it back and give it another thirty days, but do not write another guest check for the same desire. If you do, you are basically telling the Universe that you do not trust that it is coming. Feel free to write out another desire on a guest check and add it to the container. Be sure to also write your list of possibilities on how it will be delivered. Repeat this process as often as you need it.

The Universe is a real magician. It can pull far better things from its hat than white rabbits. The difference is that we, as humans, will never be privy to *how* our desires manifest. While this may seem frustrating to us control freaks, the *how* is none of our damn business. Surrender, trust, and allow the magic to unfold.

It Works!

I have worked with dozens of people on their books—I am a book coach, but I had never worked with anyone as dedicated to their beliefs as Kelly. We completed this chapter in our weekly discussions, and I was working on my plan for the next year, as we made the turn to the final quarter of the year.

"Put in your order—tell the Universe what you want," she insisted.

I was agnostic at best about the concept that the Universe provides. Yes, I knew from personal experience that you get back what you put out, whether you can see the waves or attitude, it does come back. What was there to lose? I printed an 8 x 10 of the Guest Check included in this chapter, and told the Universe that I want at least two clients a month through the next year. It was September fifteenth, and by month's end, I had two new clients for October, and another two lined up for November.

I will acknowledge that they were not delivered gift wrapped, I did have to make some effort to secure them, but I got the results. As this book goes to print, we are well into the new year, and I can tell you that at least two clients have been showing up for each month, not gift wrapped and not always ready to start on the first of the month, but they are here, and we are working on their books. Thank you, Kelly.

From Les (the book coach)

Date	Amount	Guests	Server	123456

Guest Check

Date	Table	Guests	Server	123456

APPT - SOUP/SAL - ENTREE - VEG/POT - DESSERT - BEV

	Tax	
	Total	
Thank You - Please Come Again		

TMG3616

CHAPTER 13

Divine Timing

Life is what happens while we are busy making other plans. ~ John Lennon

I've been a teacher for over twenty years. I live by bells and schedules. If my first period begins at 8:03 a.m., I can't get to the room at 8:04. When you are managing a room of teenagers, you can't be late. Teachers are the most punctual people you'll ever meet. We are conditioned to begin or dismiss when the bell rings. And while it is critical to run a school efficiently and effectively, it wreaks havoc on weekends, holidays, and summer breaks. My body is conditioned to eat and pee at certain times. Sleeping in? What's that? The point is, time holds me hostage for about one hundred and ninety days of my life. So this concept of Divine timing was one of the most challenging concepts for me to master.

While most people can't go anywhere without their phones, I can't go anywhere without my passion planner. I schedule meetings and appointments in fifteen-minute increments, so I live basically minute-to-minute. Watches and day planners are human inventions to try to manipulate time into our constructs. They are tools to structure and take control of our lives. While we can make appointments with the doctor or dentist, the Universe challenges us to stand in line and wait for our manifestation. And wait. And sometimes, wait even longer. The Universe, on the other hand, is on its own schedule. It's unfolding exactly as it should.

Divine timing is the belief that everything that happens in your life occurs at precisely the right moment. It may not feel or look like the way you want it, but you must trust that it is happening exactly as it should. Remember, you are a spiritual being having a human experience. Time is man-made.

Becoming a mother taught me about Divine timing. Because I am a teacher, I thought I was going to plan my perfect pregnancy and delivery date. I decided I would have the baby in the summer since I have summers off. Perfect, right? *Wrong*! The Universe had other plans. I didn't get pregnant when I wanted. In fact, my daughter was born five weeks prematurely, in January.

But guess what? It was better than I could have planned. Because of the complications, I was given additional paid leave. Although I had to return to work, it was only for a few weeks, and then I had the entire summer off. Because I'd had my baby in January, my body was completely healed by summertime. As an additional bonus, my daughter began daycare at eight-months-old, as opposed to only two-months-old, if my own timing had worked out. There were many blessings, even though I initially freaked out when that pregnancy test came back positive and I realized I was going to deliver a winter baby.

Apparently, I didn't fully grasp the lesson the first time, so the Universe did what every good teacher should do: teach the same content differently. I was teaching at a school in Pennsylvania and was very unhappy. Morale was low, and the work environment was becoming more and more toxic. To top it off, the pressure of teaching to the standardized tests was reaching an all-time high. Just let me teach, I seethed, but no. Instead, I was scrutinized by how well my students performed on one annual test. I was beginning to burn out. It wasn't fair to my students, and I knew I needed a change.

At the time, I had just finished up a supervisory certificate in Curriculum and Instruction, but I decided I would rather poke my eyes out, than sit in a district office analyzing boring data. I also knew that I did not want to become a principal. Managing faculty and staff were worse than herding cats, and I didn't have the filter to deal with difficult parents. Because my daughters attended private school in preschool and kindergarten, and I had directed the summer program for a few years, I decided to look into working for a private school. More leadership opportunities would still allow me to keep one foot in the classroom, but still challenge myself as an educational leader. It was also clear to me that I was ready to move away from Pennsylvania to somewhere where I didn't have to shovel snow!

So, as I taught you at the beginning, I took the first step and asked the Universe, "What would it take to work in a private school?" The next thing I knew, I was having dinner with the principal of a private school, to whom I was connected by a mutual friend. Within a few weeks, she had helped me to get accepted by a placement agency that (I hoped) would find me the perfect job. Only a few months later, I was flying to Florida to interview for a teaching position.

This hiring process was completely different than what I experienced in public school. I was flown, all expenses paid, to interview for a job. I felt like a celebrity! The head of the department invited my husband and me out to dinner the evening before the interview. We had been emailing back and forth, and I couldn't wait to meet him in person! I was still flying high (pun intended) and then he started dropping truth bomb after truth bomb about some issues with this position and the school. Morale was low. There was a high turnaround recently within the department. It sounded exactly like everything that was going on in my current school. Dinner finished and my husband and I drove back to the hotel. My husband vocalized what I didn't want to say aloud: *this wasn't the job for me.*

The next morning, I arrived at the school and delivered a kick-ass lesson. One of the students whispered to me, "You're doing a great job." Following that, the formal interview with the committee and the principal couldn't have gone better. In fact, the principal talked to me as if I was hired without officially offering me the position. But the pit in my stomach weighed heavily, and the sense that this was all wrong, was relentless. Our dinner conversation played over and over in my head. Red flag after red flag.

Over the next few days, my husband and I had serious conversations about moving to Florida. I didn't care that the department chair basically told me to run and not take this job. I was so hell-bent on getting out of my current situation that I was ignoring every warning signal from the Universe that this was not the right time. This was not the job.

A few days later, when an official offer for the position was extended, I declined it reluctantly. This was my chance to move, to work in a private school, to get out of a toxic environment, and I just let it go. I swore that I was making a big mistake. Following this experience, I had thirteen other interviews. I didn't get a single offer. In fact, I never even passed the first step of the phone interview. I really felt like I had blown my chances. I spent a lot of days pissed-off at the Universe.

However, in retrospect, if I had taken that job in Florida, I would have most likely missed out on job opportunities in Hawai'i. The Universe knew best, which is why it intervened. Its plan protected me from going from the frying pan into the fire. Incidentally, the man who interviewed me left a few months later and accepted a position at another school.

I realize now, of course, that the job wasn't meant for me. As a family, we weren't ready to move at that point. There were still many lessons I needed to learn: one was trusting in Divine timing. I now realize that when an opportunity or a manifestation doesn't come to fruition, it is truly a blessing in disguise. There really is a plan and a timing that is far better than any I could conjure up.

As an Aries, I have never been a patient person. I want things when I want them. These experiences taught me to be more patient. The saying "all good things come to those who wait" is so true. It also strengthened my faith. I can trust that when something doesn't manifest, it is because it was not for my highest good. I believe—and know—that there is something better ahead that I am not privy to at this moment. It will be revealed in Divine timing.

Inspired Assignment

Divine timing may seem like an abstract concept, but here are some physical exercises to try:

1. Reflect.

   In your journal, write about a time in your life when you didn't get something that you really believe you wanted. Reflect on these questions:

   - What did you want?
   - How did you feel at the time when it didn't happen?
   - What may have happened if your desire had come
     to fruition?

- What were the signs and red flags that the Universe showed you, that you may have ignored?
- How do you feel now that you have hindsight?
- What was the blessing in disguise?

2. Learn patience.

Find an activity that requires patience and focus, like knitting, fishing, or playing chess. Commit to trying one of these for a month. Most of the time, impatience is a symptom of an underlying emotion that you need to uncover. A lot of the time, that emotion is fear. You're afraid that if your manifestation doesn't happen right now, there will be even more significant repercussions. If you're feeling fearful or anxious, those are low vibrations, and the Universe will only match those with more fear and anxiety. Examine the root of those emotions.

3. Ditch the plan.

I understand the need to prepare in some situations. Here in Hawai'i, we have to prepare for Hurricane season. But there are many times in our lives when we try to over-schedule and over plan. My husband and I plan very little when we go on vacation. He *hates* itineraries. When we first got married, it drove me bonkers; however, because of his "go with the flow," spontaneous attitude, I have gotten to see waterfalls off the beaten path, driven on crazy back roads, and explored quaint towns that most people have never heard of. We have also driven all night long because we couldn't find a hotel room. We would have missed out on so many adventures, though, if we'd planned every detail and minute of our vacations.

Think of the Universe as your personal crossing guard. Sometimes it's safe to cross. Other times you need to wait your turn because the cars have the right of way. Sometimes you can't see what's around the corner, and you've just been spared from becoming road pizza. Trust that the Universe will allow you to cross at the safest time.

CHAPTER 14

Surrendering to Resistance

Try something different—surrender. ~ Rumi

I had no control. I had to trust that the airplane and the parachute gear were inspected carefully. I had to rely on my instructor to pull the chute open at the right moment. I learned what true surrender was when I went skydiving.

To me, the word *surrender*, means releasing your fears and control. Another word you may use is *trust*. The word surrender seems to conjure up a feeling of weakness, but the surrender I am referring to is the strength to trust entirely in the Universe manifesting as it should. This is not surrendering as in weakness. Problems arise when we try to force the Universe to manifest our ways; that's what causes resistance.

An ocean or a stream flows the way it wants; you cannot change it. Look at the tremendous power that water has, and look at what it does with that power. The Grand Canyon was cut by a tiny river. The water didn't stop when it hit a rock or ran into resistance. It found a way to continue flowing. Think about how powerful your manifestations can be when you let them flow as they should. You have a choice: are you the river or the rock?

One of my best friends had gone skydiving just a few months after I got married. It had always been on my bucket list. She wanted me to go with her, but my husband begged me not to go. He said, "I can't be a widower only weeks after marrying you." Awww, so sweet, right?! Well, at the time, I was kind of angry, but I respected his wishes. Instead, I went to watch and support her. When I saw her body plummeting from the sky, I knew I *would* do that someday, too!

Almost a decade later, the Universe served up another chance. My family and I were at a wedding reception for a relative when my cell phone rang. It was from a former student I had taught when she was in eighth grade. She and her family became dear friends after she graduated from high school. At first, I declined the call, assuming that she just wanted to chat. Immediately, she texted, asking if I could talk for only a few minutes because she needed to ask me something time-sensitive. I apologized to the people at the table and called her back.

She and her mom had found a Groupon to go skydiving. She said that her mother was turning a milestone birthday (a woman never reveals her age) and really wanted to try it. The coupon was for four people, and the deal would expire that night. My former student had gone skydiving a few times, and knew that it was on my bucket list, which is why she thought to call and ask me. My mind began to churn! The problem was, we'd need one more person.

Across the reception table, I spied my brother. I said, "Hey, Mike. Wanna go skydiving?" He didn't hesitate. "Yeah, I'll go!" Oh, I also checked-in with the hubby, thinking I'd be met with the same *hard no* I had gotten a decade prior. Instead, he surprised me. He looked at me and said, "Do what you want. I know you've wanted to do this." Marriage had taught him "happy wife, happy life." We bought the Groupon immediately, and miraculously found a date that we could all meet.

On August first, my mom, husband, kids, and brother packed into our van and drove to the tiny local airport. On route, cars honked at us because we'd decorated the van windows with messages like "Skydiving or bust" and "gone skydiving." My daughters had drawn pictures of me skydiving, and my youngest wrote, "I hope you don't die, Mommy!" Pumped full of adrenaline, reality finally hit me that I may be looking death right in its eyes. My poor mother was about to watch both of her children jump out of a perfectly good airplane. I was beginning to freak out!

Then, it was time. We boarded the tiny puddle jumper, tethered to our instructors with passenger harnesses. (By the way, I need to give a shout out to Michael from New Zealand. He was not only an excellent instructor, but easy on the eyes, if you know what I mean...aside from my husband, of course!) As the plane ascended higher and higher into the sky, I actually began to relax. There was no turning back at this point. I said a quiet prayer and then I did the only thing I could do: *trust*. At that moment, I trusted I would be safe. I believed that I would land safely. I knew I'd be okay.

The hatch opened and I looked down. Everyone tells me that they can't believe I looked down, but oddly it didn't scare me. I saw the beautiful landscape below, and within seconds, like a bird, I was soaring above it.

It wasn't until several months later that it hit me. Skydiving taught me several lessons. The Universe used it as a vehicle to show me how to release control, and what it means to surrender completely. It allowed me to be genuinely vulnerable, by literally throwing my hands into the air, waiting to receive. Although it may seem like an oxymoron, during my freefall, I felt a calm and peace that I've never experienced before. When my butt glided gently back onto the Earth and landed, I was grounded in knowing that the Universe provides both roots and wings.

You may be thinking, "There is *no* way I am ever going skydiving, so I guess I just wasted my time reading this chapter." While I still highly recommend the experience, I totally understand that it is not feasible or desirable for the majority of people. You can experience complete surrender without jumping out of an airplane. Instead of experiencing a physical surrender, there is a process you can try to get there mentally; that is key!

Surrendering is a difficult concept for many. Before I learned how to quickly get into the last of the three powerful universal laws described by Abraham Hicks, the Law of Allowing, which is essentially to just relax and "go with the flow," I was an Instapot. All of my emotions, limiting beliefs, and what-ifs would cook to the point that if I didn't release the steam valve, the damn thing would explode. I don't recommend losing your temper, but if that's what it takes for you to surrender, do it! Get mad. Punch a pillow. Scream. Release the emotions and walk away.

Inspired Assignment

The first step in surrendering, is to revisit the cursed *"H" is for How* chapter. You must give up control in order to fully surrender. It's actually our ego we need to let go of. While our ego is trying to keep us safe, it's actually creating resistance. Although we are deliberate creators, we must trust that we don't have to create everything. When we can fully let go of *how,* miracles will happen.

The next step is to alter your state of being. Right now, stop and think of something you want to manifest. What limiting thoughts or beliefs are bubbling up? Bring awareness to each of these thoughts. Thank your ego and say aloud, "I trust Divine timing. I let go of the how. I surrender." Say it as many times, and as often, as you need to. As Gabby Berstein teaches, when you think you have surrendered, surrender more.

If you're asking, "I let go, now what?" I need to drop a truth bomb on you. If you need to ask that question, you haven't truly surrendered. Go back to step one and have (what I call) a come-to-Jesus talk with your ego. Your ego is not in control. Give your power to your higher self and allow it to work in your favor. And remember, sometimes things will not go in your favor. Do not resist that! Surrender to the fact that the new path may lead you to a totally different outcome that is better than the one you thought you wanted.

Surrender is not giving up or giving in. Surrendering is not a weakness. The Universe is not your enemy; *you* may be your own worst enemy. Stop fighting yourself. The war is not with the Universe; the battle is within yourself. Put down your flag and allow the Universe to raise it in victory for you!

CHAPTER 15

Aligning to Your Purpose

It doesn't take time; it just takes alignment. ~ Abraham Hicks

Like most college kids, I had to work a part-time job during summer breaks and holidays to help defray the costs. I have had a variety of positions in fast food and retail since I was fourteen years old. The summer before attending college, my mother suggested I work with her at the candy factory she has worked at for decades. It seemed ideal. I would make a good wage, work only Monday to Friday from 7:00 am to 3:00 pm, no weekends, it was temporary, and I could eat all the candy I wanted during my shifts. I was living the real-life version of *Charlie and the Chocolate Factory*! Um, no! *I was wrong!*

On my first day, the boss handed me a hairnet and smock and assigned me to a "line." My job was to inspect the candy as it came down the belt and remove any pieces that didn't meet the standard. Sounds easy, right? Nope. That belt was moving at a rapid clip and I couldn't keep up. Soon, the candy began piling up, creating a blockage, and then the line shut down. Now, I was in a real-life episode of *I Love Lucy*, where Lucy and Ethel can't wrap the candy fast enough as it flies down the belt. (By the way, if you haven't seen that *Lucy* episode, I recommend you search for it on YouTube!) Within minutes, I was scolded by the mechanic who had to fix the machine I'd just broken. After that, they moved me around to several other lines and jobs; I failed at all of them.

I cried every day after work. This job was hard! I thought about my mom, who endured these mundane tasks every single day of her life; she never complained. In fact, she even enjoyed many aspects of her job. I began to question my life's purpose. This job was clearly not in alignment with my skill set or purpose. There was no way I could do these tasks day after day. My soul tank was empty. After a week, I quit and began working as a playground leader. I declared English education as my major, and knew that this was much more in alignment with what I wanted to do as a career.

My mother grew up in a previous generation where the beliefs around work were much different than exist now. You worked to make a living. If you happened to enjoy and love what you did, that was a bonus, but the purpose of working was to get paid—Period. No one believed or practiced that you could actually make money from what you loved to do. The motivation was to work now, so you could retire, and *then* you could do what you wanted. Women also had very few choices where they could work if they were not stay-at-home mothers. Most were teachers, nurses, or factory workers. Since learning about deliberate creation and manifestation, I don't hold these beliefs.

Instead, I believe we come into this world with a purpose. It is our journey to identify what that is. I am not criticizing factory workers, or any job for that matter. We need people like my mother, or we wouldn't have chocolate—*gasp*, automobiles, or screws that hold our windows in place. If you enjoy your work, I applaud you. I am grateful for these people because we need them to do these jobs. I'm referring to those people who know they have a higher purpose but are not acting upon it. My point is, if you hate your job, do *not* waste another day. Many of my clients stay in situations because it's comfortable, like their favorite pair of jeans. It's too scary to pursue a passion because what if they fail? Don't sit there, shaking your head, saying, "I can't. I need the money, the benefits, the retirement." These are all thoughts that became excuses and are now beliefs; thoughts can be changed.

One of my former students accepted her parents' beliefs as her own, and it almost cost her life. To protect her privacy, let's call her Arden (another one of my favorite names, and it's another Shakespearean reference! Have I mentioned that I love Shakespeare?). Arden was a talented artist and poet, but grew up in a strict family where the expectation was that she would pursue a career in math or science. Although her school had a fantastic art program with cutting edge technology, Arden was not even allowed to take an art elective.

Art had been a vehicle she used to cope with depression. As a child, she painted, sketched, wrote, and expressed a voice that was silenced, often by her parents. She was self-taught. Over the years, she was ridiculed and scolded for making art when she should be studying. Art was her passion. She lived it, and breathed it daily, until denying that part of her became so painful she almost took her life.

One day Arden shared her story, addressing an audience of other juniors and seniors. As she ended her speech with a poem that she'd written about the day she tried to take her life, I looked around the room. Many students wiped away tears, and she received a standing ovation. I approached her afterward and asked her if she would be willing to come to my office to chat.

Weeks went by, but finally, one day, Arden came and plopped herself on my couch in tears. She was in the process of applying to college and had gotten into a fight with her parents. She wanted to apply as an art major, but they insisted if she didn't choose business as her major, they would not pay her tuition. They believed that becoming an artist would never be financially profitable, and it was a waste of time and money. They insisted that she needed to focus on a career that would give her money and to stop the art nonsense.

It is not my job or expertise to give college counseling advice, so I began a discussion on what I know about manifesting. I told Arden to apply for business as her parents demanded, but I also taught her that when we align with our soul's purpose, the Universe will move mountains for us. I told her that we need to set the intention, and then take action in any way we can. In her case, that meant finding any opportunity to do art, showcase her work, and meet other artists. I encouraged her to keep making art and writing poetry.

"There is no way my parents are ever going to let me change my major, Mrs. Weaver," she said. She had a lot of resistance around how it was going to happen.

I said, "It's not up to your parents, you've given it to the Universe now."

Arden went off to college. Then a few weeks before her winter break, she texted me, inviting me to have lunch, so we could catch up. Her text read, "You won't believe what is happening!"

I learned that Arden had done everything I suggested. Right before she left for college, she had been designing t-shirts and selling them. It was wildly successful. Within a month of being at college, she set up at an art fair on campus and sold the t-shirts. A man approached the booth and exclaimed over the designs. He assumed she was a senior art major, ready to launch a career, and here she was just a freshman! He was an alumnus and he wanted to help her, so he offered to create a website to sell the shirts. It was a five-thousand-dollar investment that he gifted to her! Arden continues to sell the shirts, but many more doors have opened for her since then. Her other art pieces have been featured in galleries. As a result, her parents have come around to supporting her as an art major; she transferred to a prestigious art college where she is thriving.

When Arden aligned with her passion and purpose, the Universe rushed in to support her in several different ways. First, Arden received monetary compensation from the sales of the t-shirts, which enabled her to help defray some of her college costs. Next, she received a free website which attracted more customers and followers. The Universe helped her to heal her relationship with her parents and they have become her biggest cheerleaders and supporters.

They have finally had several heart-to-heart conversations, and Arden learned they were projecting their own fears and inadequacies onto her. Arden's parents struggled financially and didn't like their jobs. Their intention was to protect her from the challenges they had endured, so that she wouldn't have to struggle as they did. Her actions demonstrated to them that she could monetize her passion and work in a career she loves. Both could exist simultaneously.

Most importantly, Arden healed herself. Her depression completely diminished; she now has a healthy and loving relationship with her parents. She is thriving at her new college and has attracted a tribe of people who love and support her as an artist. As a result, doors continue to open for her. The Universe uses Arden as an instrument to inspire other budding artists who struggle with depression and self-worth. This opportunity has allowed her to continue her work as a spoken word poet.

How do you know if you are in alignment? You know you are in alignment when things flow smoothly and effortlessly. Arden created art; she didn't stop because her parents wanted her to. As a result, the Universe rewarded her action by giving her money, resources, and opportunities to pursue her purpose. Arden reminded me that day at lunch, that when we are in alignment with our soul's purpose, the Universe takes the puzzle pieces and completes the picture for us. It is always working for our highest good.

Inspired Assignment

As a Law of Attraction coach, I find that most of the clients who come to work with me are searching for their soul's purpose. Sadly, they have no idea and are looking for clarity. *What the heck should they do with their lives?* I often ask them this question: What would you do if money was not an object? Recently, I read somewhere that you should have three hobbies: one that makes money, one that allows you to be creative, and one that is relaxing or mindless. This exercise will help you identify all three, and perhaps even align you to your purpose.

Try to avoid being judgmental and critical of yourself as you do this process. I can just hear some of you objecting, "I can't do that. I have a family to take care of, I don't have the money, I can't be away from my house that long, I have kids... blah, blah, blah." This is supposed to be a fun brainstorming exercise. Be that four-year-old who is fearless and full of dreams. She doesn't question how she will become an astronaut, doctor, and dog trainer all at the same time. She's not concerned about how much it will cost or how it will all unfold. You don't need to question *how*; your job right now is to identify the *what*. Remember, the Universe will take care of the how.

1. Make a list of all of the things you enjoy doing.

2. Select your top choice. Brainstorm various ways that you could monetize this passion. Dream big here. Even if it seems silly or impossible, write it down!

Example: my neighbor loves going to spas and writing. How in the world could she combine these two seemingly unrelated passions? She travels the world, experiencing the top-rated spas and writing reviews on them for Conde Nast! She found a way to enjoy spa treatments while getting paid to be pampered!

3. Take a step, *any* step. It does not have to be all or nothing. You don't—and shouldn't necessarily—have to leave your nine-to-five. It could develop into a full-time career, but at least it becomes a hobby you enjoy that gives you a return. It is still winning! If you like taking photos, offer to photograph a friend for free in exchange for a testimonial. That one action could open the door to a plethora of clients who love your work. I wanted to be a speaker, so I called the local rotary club and offered to come and speak for free. They said yes, but suggested that I wait until my book had been published, so that I could sell it there and have a book signing! Turns out it wouldn't be a "free" speech after all. Don't you just love the Universe?

As Mark Twain said, "The two most important days in your life are the day you are born, and the day you find out why."

Update!
After writing this chapter, I received this text message from Arden. "Oh, I am not sure if it would be worth mentioning, but as of right now, I am on track to have saved up enough money to pay off all of my student loans right after I graduate—all from money made off of my arts endeavors."

From Arden
Arden also has garnered an impressive social meeting following on a few platforms.

CHAPTER 16

"A" is for Act as If

My boss told me, "Dress for the job you want, not the job you have." Now I'm sitting in a disciplinary meeting dressed as Wonder Woman. ~ Meme

Step Five: The final "A" is for Act as If. I have wanted to be a teacher since I could talk. I remember lining up my stuffed animals in a row in front of my chalkboard (no whiteboards or high-tech screens back then) and teaching them how to write letters and to solve simple math problems. One day, one of my stuffed animal bears fell over and I practiced scolding him so that I would have experience with my own students, who surely wouldn't sit so attentively. Let me tell you, that practice of scolding came in handy many times over my teaching career!

In Kindergarten, my friends would often come to my house and we would play "mommy." I would raid my grandmother's closet for high heels and a purse so I could look the part. Nowadays as moms we are lucky to be dressed and out of PJ's let alone wearing high heels, but remember I was only about five years old, and I had watched too many episodes of *Leave it to Beaver*. We would take our baby dolls for long walks in their strollers, or stop by the playground and push them on the swings. We would read, and sing, and talk with our babies for hours.

Most children play pretend games. Our modern kids spend hours gaming in virtual reality fantasy worlds, where they can try on many different identities and personalities, and be whomever they chose. Somewhere along the way, we grow up and stop using our imaginations. We are told to snap back into reality. We give up on our dreams because we are told that's not realistic. It's a shame, because we disconnect from the power of manifestation, and don't realize how easily we can plug back in. The Universe doesn't distinguish between reality and fantasy, so the more that you *act as if* you have your desire, the faster the Universe will deliver it to you. It may have taken decades, but I became a teacher and a mother. I know it's not a coincidence. I acted as if I was already a teacher and a mother, and the Universe made it happen...in Divine timing.

I manifested my dream job in Hawai'i by acting as if I was already in the role. Sick and tired of shoveling snow and freezing temperatures, I signed up with a private school placement agency. I decided to leave public school because test scores became more important than my students. I became a teacher to make a difference in the lives of children, not to teach to a test that doesn't even truly measure their abilities. I also completed an administrative internship to pursue a leadership role in a middle school. The agency's purpose was to match educators and administrators with potential private schools. During the application process, I was able to identify several preferences, and one of those preferences was geographical location. I clicked on Hawai'i, and a few months later, I was sitting in front of my boss.

This particular agency held recruitment fairs throughout the country, so I decided to attend the one in Florida. It was actually a cool and nerve-wracking process. I received a daily calendar, and schools would populate it if they wanted to interview me. I could view all of the schools and their openings, but I really couldn't control whether or not a school chose to interview me. I was thrilled to see that my calendar filled quickly. My heart nearly stopped, though, when I read the last time slot of the day; the school from Hawai'i wanted to interview me! What a way to end my day. But it got better. They were not looking for a teacher; they were looking for a Director of Student Activities. Although the job description was incredibly vague, I knew immediately that this was the absolute perfect role for me.

Because that was indeed the only position I was interested in, I spent every free minute researching the school. I visited the website, where I introduced myself to the students I saw and read about. I envisioned myself in the classrooms, sitting at a football game, and walking the grounds of the beautiful campus. Every person I met, I introduced myself, "Aloha, I'm Kelly, the new Director of Student Activities."

By the time I got to my interview, I didn't just know the job was mine, I felt it in my entire being. I sat down for what I described as my speed-session interview, and I knew when they shook my hand at the end, that I would be hired.

On my youngest daughter's birthday, they called me to set up an interview. This private school thing was new to me, so I didn't realize that they were flying me to Hawai'i to do the interview. The interview went so well that when I got home, I told my immediate family to pack their bags because we would be moving to Hawai'i. I had just had dinner with my besties, basically telling them I was moving because I was sure I had gotten the job, when my phone pinged that I'd received an email as I walked to my car. I did *not* get the job!

Devastation wasn't even a strong enough word to describe how I felt. I was furious! Sobbing in the dark of my car, I kept reading the email over and over again. I screamed and pounded on the steering wheel, demanding an explanation. I knew this job was mine. I felt it. I had acted *as if* in every single way. *What the heck happened?*

At that moment, I threw in the proverbial towel. Then, about two weeks later, I got another call. There was an unexpected opening in the English department of the same school in Hawai'i to teach eighth and ninth grade. One of the English teachers, who had served on the interviewing committee, apparently really liked me and asked if they could contact me to see if I would consider this position. I had mentioned in my interview that I was ready to move out of the classroom, so they didn't know if I would be interested.

When I told my husband about the offer, he said, "We are not moving six thousand miles away for you to teach English; you already do that here."

I looked him in the eye and said, "I understand, but that Student Activities job is mine. I know it, and I feel it. Something is going to happen, and it is mine."

I interviewed, got offered the English position, and accepted the job. It was the biggest blessing in disguise. It gave me a year to learn the culture, the students, and the traditions. I got to know the faculty and staff. I was there to participate in all of the activities, assemblies, and events. The woman they'd chosen instead became a dear friend and my greatest spiritual running buddy. Almost a year after I was hired, she confided to me that she was moving back to California. Unfortunately, because she hadn't had the time that I'd had to learn the ropes, it just wasn't a fit for her. A few weeks later, the Director also announced his resignation. There were now two positions open, and in 2015, I was hired as one of the new Co-Directors. When I answer the phone, "Student Activities Office, this is Kelly," I often smile and remember that by acting *as if,* I created my reality.

Dressing for and acting the part of the desire is preparation for the manifestation. When you align with the feeling of your desire, you align with the frequency of your desire. By acting as if you manifested your wish, you align with the vibrational frequency of gratitude, which allows it to be delivered almost instantaneously. You should be questioning that last statement if you've been reading any of this book carefully because my manifestation wasn't instantaneous, or even fast. The point is, the Universe *always* knows what is best for your highest good. Timing is everything. Sometimes, when we are rejected, or don't get what we think we want, the Universe was actually protecting us. If I had gotten the job the first time, I probably would have ended up like my friend and had to move back to the mainland. The Universe always has your back.

Inspired Assignment

Do you remember the opening of the TV show, *The Simpsons*? Bart is writing the same sentence over and over again on the chalkboard as his punishment. Well, you're going to be writing something similar, except you're not being punished. You will be rewarded immensely if you follow the steps. There is a Law of Attraction process to help you "act as if." It is called the 5x55 process. Unlike some of the other processes I have taught you, this one has a few rules.

Use a journal, notebook, or paper. For five days, you will write a statement of gratitude fifty-five times, acting as if your desire has already manifested. You can use a pen, pencil, marker, or crayon, but you must physically write it. You cannot type it or just say it aloud. You must write the statement exactly the same fifty-five times for five straight days. If you miss a day, you must start over at day one. If your statement was: "Thank you, Universe, for my brand-new red BMW convertible," using the 5x55 process, you would write that statement fifty-five times for five consecutive days. It doesn't matter if you use a pencil one day and pen the next. It doesn't matter if you write it in the morning one day and in the evening another day. The primary rule is that you write the exact statement fifty-five times for five consecutive days.

Example:
1. *Thank you, Universe, for the $5,000 to pay for my trip to Paris.*
2. *Thank you, Universe, for the $5,000 to pay for my trip to Paris.*
3. *Thank you, Universe, for the $5,000 to pay for my trip to Paris.*
.....
55. *Thank you, Universe, for the $5,000 to pay for my trip to Paris.*

How often can you do this? The answer is, anytime you want to manifest your desires, however, you should never repeat the same statement. Remember, you already acted as if you received your desire and thanked the Universe, so if you merely write the same statement, you are basically saying you don't trust that the Universe will deliver. You're not really acting as if you have already received it. Let go of the dreaded *how* and wait for it to come to you in Divine timing.

I have used this 5x55 process twice. Both times I asked for specific amounts of money, and both times I received precisely what I asked for. The cool part was how it manifested. I could never have dreamed up the ways in which that money came to me. Remember: the *how* is none of your damn business!

CHAPTER 17

Self-Care

Self-care is giving the world the best of you,
instead of what's left of you. ~ Katie Reed

When I was fourteen years old, I responded to a classified ad in the newspaper. A family was seeking a babysitter for Saturdays and other occasional days. I was hired, and still have a relationship with the family to this day! Bragging moment: I taught the oldest boy how to tie his shoes.

Around the same time, another family hired me to sit for them so they could go on regular dates. They paid really well, and I usually babysat two or three times a month. One night, the mom and I were in the kitchen, prepping food for the kids before they would head out to their dinner. She gave me a piece of advice that I silently rejected until I became the stressed out, exhausted mom myself.

She said, "Kelly, if you ever get married and have children, be sure that you make time to go on dates with your husband and by yourself. Your marriage will depend on it. It's the foundation. You come first. Then your husband, then your children. Someday your children will grow up and leave the house. You don't want to be staring at your husband, wondering who he is and who you are. You're not just parents raising kids. You're lovers, partners, and people with your own needs too."

I admit, I thought she was crazy. You need to absolutely put your children first, I thought. How selfish they were! I was certain that my kids would always be the center of my world. Why have children if they weren't your first priority? Then I got married and became a working mom. I was putting everyone's needs before my own. One day while hiding in the bathroom crying, trying to get a moment of peace, I remembered her sage advice.

As women, we tend to put everyone's needs before our own. We worry not only about others' needs, but we also worry about how others perceive us. We spread ourselves way too thin and sacrifice our own health, needs, and desires. Then we disguise our resentment and anger in martyrdom. By not taking care of ourselves, we disconnect from the frequency of the Universe and manifest what we don't want: more stress, worry, pressure, and anxiety.

Self-care is not selfish. It's essential. Self-care is taking care of yourself in every aspect: physically, emotionally, mentally, and spiritually. It does not have to be expensive or elaborate. Not everyone wants a massage or a weekend in Tahoe. There is a reason that flight attendants tell you to put your oxygen mask on first before you help someone else. If your cup is empty, you have nothing to give. A car won't run on empty. Why do we, especially women, believe we can?

Kristin (her name is changed for privacy) thought she could run on empty, until she landed herself in the hospital, not once, but three times. Kristin seemed to have it all. She and her husband were happily married. With news that their second baby, a girl, was on the way, they traded their apartment in the city for a single-family home in the country. Although the move added a commute, they didn't mind it because it actually allowed them to spend time together.

Two years later, Kristin headed to a doctor's appointment before work. The pregnancy test confirmed she was expecting. Life was absolutely perfect! She called her husband on her way to the office and they cried happy tears. Little did she know that in just thirty minutes, those tears of happiness would turn to devastation.

As soon as she got into her office, her secretary was waiting for her. Before Kristin could share her great news, her secretary stopped her and told her that the supervisor needed to talk to Kristin right away. From her expression, Kristin knew something was terribly wrong.

"Please, have a seat," the supervisor offered.

"What's wrong? You're scaring me?" Kristin asked.

"I'm very sorry, Kristin. I know this seems very sudden. The company is in financial distress and we need to downsize. We need to let you go."

She cried, "What? I literally just came from my doctor's office. I'm expecting a baby, and now you're telling me I don't have a job? This is a bad joke, right?!"

"Oh, Kristin. Congratulations," her supervisor acknowledged. "Wow, I'm so sorry, but no, this isn't a joke."

Tears streamed down her cheeks, this time from anger, sadness, and gut-wrenching fear. How would they pay the mortgage? They would surely lose the house. How would they take care of their son and this baby on the way? Why was this happening? What was she going to tell her husband?

After clearing out her desk, Kristin headed home. It was while she was in the car that she had a major epiphany. The Universe just helped her clear space for what she had been trying to do for the past few years. She could now finally start her own online business. Over the years, she had been trying to build it as a side hustle, but marriage, a baby, a new house, and her career prevented her from growing it. As Kristin adjusted her rearview mirror and caught a glimpse of the road behind her, she drove with determination into her new life.

...Until she hit the first of many detours.

Her husband got a promotion, which should have been great news, but it kept him away from home a lot. Here she was, sick as a dog for most of the pregnancy, while trying to build a business with a toddler underfoot. Month after month went by, with no income from her business, and then the baby was born. Debt piled as high as the stress. They had no family close by to help. One day Kristin began having chest pains and couldn't catch her breath. She was certain she'd had a heart attack.

At the emergency room, she was carefully evaluated and diagnosed with anxiety and depression, determining that her chest pain had been due to a panic attack. The doctor gave her a prescription and encouraged her to go to therapy, but he also asked her something completely unexpected that, when she told me later, blew my mind. He asked what her self-care practice looked like? Of course, she told the doctor she didn't have time for self-care or therapy. His next words really pissed her off, "Ok, well, if you don't make time for yourself," he warned, "I guarantee I'll be seeing you again soon." He wasn't wrong. Within just three months, she saw him two more times for severe panic attacks. Finally, she took his advice and found a therapist, her first step toward self-care.

When Kristin learned to put on her own oxygen mask first, her whole world began to change. The business started to grow, the children began to thrive, her relationship with her husband strengthened, and he began helping her more with the home and kids, which allowed her more time for herself. She learned that by keeping her cup full, and giving from the saucer, this not only benefited her physical and emotional health, but it actually allowed her to give so much more to her family and others.

Kristin also unpacked some beliefs she harbored about her Protestant work ethic. She didn't have to sacrifice herself or her needs. Work didn't have to be demanding and difficult as she was taught as a child. Burnout was not a badge of honor.

Her children also modeled a vital lesson that we can all learn; play is so important. We think it's reserved for children, but play naturally raises our vibration. I'm not suggesting you have to go swing from the monkey bars or play dodgeball, but find an activity that brings you joy. Kristin's children love games, so they began to implement a weekly family game night, complete with pizza and ice cream. Kristin admitted that the first few times were challenging, because she was worried about the pile of laundry that needed to be folded, or the paperwork piled on her desk, but seeing her children and husband laughing made her relax into the moment. For a few hours, she could let go and have fun. Guess what?! The more fun she had, the more fun and joy she attracted.

Inspired Assignment

Self-care is the greatest act of self-love you can give yourself. It doesn't have to be elaborate, expensive, or time-consuming. A little goes a long way. When I first began a conscious effort to focus on my own self-care, I designated Sundays as Self-Care Sundays. Each week, I would go live on my Facebook page and share my self-care practice for that particular day. It inspired some of my viewers to begin their own practices. If you don't have a regular exercise, I challenge you to implement a self-care practice each day for the next thirty days.

1. Identify your self-care practice and how long you will devote to it each day for the next thirty days. It can be anything that you enjoy that alleviates stress and is totally focused on you. It might be something as simple as going for a walk, taking a bath, meditating, journaling, or reading. The list is infinite.

2. Begin small. Dedicate five to ten minutes daily and build up as this practice becomes a habit. If you think you don't have time, I challenge you to change that story and create an affirmation: *"I have plenty of time for self-care; my needs are my priority."* Maybe you need to wake up five minutes earlier, or go to bed five minutes later. Quit watching Netflix or scrolling mindlessly on social media. You can find at least five minutes for yourself in a twenty-four-hour day.

3. Schedule it like you would any other appointment. Do *not* cancel on yourself. You wouldn't cancel something necessary like a doctor's appointment. Make this time non-negotiable. Tell your spouse, partner, or kids, that you are unavailable at this time and not to bother you. I'm serious about this. My family knows that every night before I go to bed, I read for at least fifteen minutes. It's non-negotiable. Someone better be hemorrhaging or dying if they bother mama's reading time. Even when I had a toddler and an infant, I read each night. Influenza B and childbirth may be the only times I missed my reading self-care practice.

4. Give yourself this gift daily for thirty days. As you love yourself, the Universe will love you too.

It seems counterintuitive, but when you are busiest and most stressed, that is when you need self-care the most. If you are stressed, you are resistant. Walk away from whatever is lowering your vibration, and find an activity that will bring you up the emotional guidance scale, even if it is only one degree. When you take care of yourself, the Universe will rush in to take care of you.

CHAPTER 18

Visualization

Create the highest, grandest vision possible for your life,
because you become what you believe. ~ Oprah Winfrey

For the past several years, I have hosted a "Vino and Visions" night for my soul sisters to create vision boards. I coined this phrase "Vinos and Visions," so you cannot steal it (well, if you do, you must give me credit and a case of vino)!

A vision board is a collection of pictures, images, and words that you want to manifest into your life. I begin each party by explaining the meaning of a vision board, its purpose, and how we are each about to make one. Next, I lead a meditation to open the evening so everyone is focused and grounded. And yes, we sip our wine as we create our vision board for the new year. Around the room, the energy is palpable, as we share stories about our hopes and dreams for the future.

I began this exercise because I wanted to create a safe place where my friends could be vulnerable and talk about what they longed to manifest. They know there is no judgment, and we all agree to hold space for each other's desires.

Visualization allows you to see your desires as though you have already manifested them. If you imagine you already have manifested your intentions, you train—or trick—your psyche into believing that you already possess these desires. You behave as though they have come to fruition. As I have outlined in the five steps, acting *as if* changes your energetic vibration to align with the same frequency of your desire. When like attracts like, you will hold your reality in your hand.

Consider athletes for a moment, particularly golfers. Golfers use visualization to see where the shot will land. They actually play golf in their minds before they ever hit the course. We can apply that same rule as we can see the result of what we are asking for, or what we are thinking about having. It's the technique I used to manifest meeting my longtime hero.

Since I was a little girl, I always imagined meeting Oprah in person. Every day after school, I would watch her show with my mom and grandmother. In many ways, Oprah was a virtual big sister who taught me valuable life lessons. Oprah and I share many similar experiences around family trauma and weight issues. At one point in college, I thought I would be a TV news anchor and longed to have a talk show as she did. I am fortunate to have a few Gayles in my life, too.

For three years, Oprah Winfrey had been the central image of my vision board. During one Vinos and Vision party, I declared that Oprah and I would have lunch together in her home in Maui. I envisioned her interviewing me about my book for an episode of SuperSoul Sunday. We would laugh, sip tea, and "talk story" as we say here in Hawai'i.

One holiday, some friends, who own a home in Maui, invited us to stay with them. I discovered that they actually live relatively close to Oprah's Hawaiian residence. During our visit, my friend Jen, who regularly takes walks around the island, asked me to join her. She assured me that I would love it. To my surprise, her destination was the road that led to Oprah's house!

Now, don't misunderstand me, it wasn't as if when you got to the end of the road, you could just walk up and ring her doorbell. But it was the road that Oprah and her employees used to get to her home. Jen knew how much I love Oprah, which was why she took me on that particular walk. As we strolled along, I honestly had butterflies in my stomach. What if she drove by? What would I say? I visualized the whole conversation in my head! Unfortunately, though we walked the road each day while I was visiting, we never once caught a glimpse of Oprah.

Several weeks later, my phone rang early on a Sunday morning. It was my friend Karen, who also lived on Maui and was out walking with Jen. At the time, Karen was also my boss, so I was afraid to answer the call, thinking something terrible had happened. After all, why would she be calling me on a Sunday morning?

Before I could even say hello, Karen screamed into the phone, "Oh my God, we just saw Oprah!"

Stunned, I attempted to put the pieces together. Through the screeching, I finally understood that they had been walking along that same road when Oprah drove past with Stedman in the passenger seat. Oprah said hello to them and they exchanged a few pleasantries before she went on her way. OMG! My friends not only saw Oprah, but talked to her. And she spoke to them! I felt like I was one step closer to meeting her myself. Little did I know, I was!

In late 2019, Orpah announced her Oprah's '2020 Vision' Tour with Weight Watchers. When I checked the dates and locations, I knew my dream was about to come true. I had applied to attend a conference in Philadelphia. The dates of her tour and my conference coincided so that I could attend the event in Los Angeles on February twenty-ninth: *Leap day.*

So, now I need to get a little "woo woo" on you here. First, it was a leap year, which only occurs every four years, so it was already an extraordinary day. *Leaping into 2020 with Oprah!* Second, in numerology, the number twenty-nine is a fantastic number. To explain, each number carries a vibration, so you want to reduce any number to a single digit. When you take the number twenty-nine and reduce it to a single digit, you would add two plus nine to get eleven. Eleven is actually a master number, so you don't reduce it any further. Eleven is the number of manifesting. Remember, in the signs chapter, we discussed seeing numbers like 11:11 or 8:08 on a clock?

Third, Los Angeles is the city of Angels; my own angels seemed to be guiding me there! Also, with the year being 2020, many people associate it with perfect vision. Numerologically, it reduces to the number four, which according to my favorite website *Sacred Angel Numbers*, angel number four means that your angels are around you and that you are able to call upon them for help, guidance, and assistance whenever you feel the need. You simply trust that you have all the skills, talents, and abilities to overcome any obstacles and you can achieve your highest aspirations. Angel number four also encourages you to put proper preparation into your plans and set things in motion with system and order, so I knew it was my sign to purchase that $530 conference ticket. It was worth every penny!

On February 29, 2020, I sat in auditorium seat 232 (check out that number on the angel site) at The Forum and eagerly watched Oprah take the stage. It was beyond any expectation I'd had. It was indeed a "day-long party," as she promised. For the next six glorious hours, our sold-out crowd sang, laughed, cried, and danced. Oprah walked us through a workbook she had created, and challenged us all to get a clear vision of our life. Stedman and Gayle surprised us; they had been sitting in the audience! Jennifer Lopez was the featured visionary, and Oprah interviewed her like the good old days of her talk show. No, I didn't get to meet, hug, or shake her hand that day, but I know that Oprah and I will eat a delicious, healthy lunch on her lanai after our interview on SuperSoul Sunday. I do hope you will tune in!

When I placed Oprah at the center of my vision board in 2016, I was putting my order into the Universe. I had no idea how it would manifest. I released attachment from the how and allowed the Universe to work out the details. In the same way that I wouldn't barge into the kitchen of a restaurant to see how my meal was being cooked, I waited patiently to be served.

I had also been extremely deliberate in choosing the perfect picture of Oprah to evoke a strong emotional response. I could have simply cut out her name, but it wouldn't have been nearly as powerful as the image I'd selected. Donned in a bright red dress, hands on her hips, with lips drawn in a small smile, Oprah stood confidently, gazing into the camera. Just looking at that image made me want to throw back my shoulders and stand tall, declaring that I am also a powerful woman who will make my dreams come true.

Visualization not only requires using your eyes, but it should also employ all five senses. When I visualize meeting Oprah for our lunch, I not only see the food, I taste and smell it, while Stedmon clangs pots and pans in the kitchen. I breathe the aroma of Oprah's perfume and the flowers in her garden. I hear the chirp of birds, and feel a gentle breeze, as the trade winds blow strands of hair across my face, I reach out to touch her soft hands and envelop myself in her soft embrace, as she hugs me and welcomes me into her home.

Inspired Assignment

A vision board doesn't have to be expensive or fancy. You can use a cork board, poster board, or even construction paper. I was able to find a really cool and inexpensive cork board at *Ross*. While you can make vision boards online, I do highly recommend that for this exercise you use tangible materials. There is something magical in the process of the old-school cut and paste method.

1. Gather old magazines, photos, and newspapers. Cut out pictures, words, phrases, and images that you want to manifest. The images can be a mix of concrete and abstract objects. If a picture evokes a strong feeling, go ahead and cut that out. Remember, the image should evoke a strong emotional response. There is absolutely no wrong way to do this. If there is an image you want that you cannot find in a magazine, google it and print it from your computer.

2. Don't allow self-judgment or criticism to creep in. As adults, we have such a hard time dreaming. Some people feel selfish in wanting to put pictures of money, cars, or diamond rings on their board. *Stop that.* You put on that board everything and anything your heart desires. Once, I put a diamond ring on my board, and my oldest daughter freaked out. She demanded to know why I would put a ring on there when I was happily married. I assured her that, while I still love the diamond my hubby gave during his proposal, a woman can want more bling after twenty-some years of marriage!

3. Attach the images to your vision board with thumbtacks, glue, tape, etc.

4. Place your vision board in a location where you can see it every day when you wake up, and when you go to bed.

5. Take a minute or more each time you look at it to not only see the images but to truly *feel* the vibrations they emit. What feelings rise up? Where do you feel it on your body? Smile as you look at each image. Visualize and act as if you already manifested it. The vision board is simply the tool to get you into the alignment of your desire; you need to *feel* the emotions that each picture evokes.

Not every manifestation on your vision board will come to fruition; that's ok. There may be something better for you. It may not be the right timing. If it's truly for your highest good, it will manifest. It took me half of a lifetime to see Oprah. What began as a seed, watching her on my grandparents' box television set, turned into watching her standing live on stage just several hundred feet away from me after almost thirty-five years! Dreams do come true.

P.S. And yes, this book was on my vision board too!

CHAPTER 19

The Power of Positivity

If you change the way you look at things,
the things you look at change. ~ Wayne Dyer

Imagine the scene. Cavemen are sitting in a circle around a fire that is burning brightly. Within a few seconds, the peacefulness is interrupted by a saber-toothed tiger charging at them. Chaos ensues. Some men flee, others battle it with their clubs. This is where the term fight or flight originated. Thousands of years ago, it was necessary to keep us safe. Our survival depended upon it.

Here in the twenty-first century, although there are no saber-toothed tigers actively threatening our safety, biologically, we haven't changed much. It is still part of our DNA. That's why humans, by nature, are negative beings. It is a biological response to keep us safe.

Being positive is not our natural state. But being positive is necessary for the Law of Attraction, because the law states: like attracts like. If you are negative, you will notice that more negative things come into your life. If you're positive, you will attract more positive things into your life.

Now listen, I can almost see some of you rolling your eyes. Here's another Pollyanna attitude warning me that if I complain or have a negative thought, I'll never be able to manifest anything I desire. Not true. All humans are both positive and negative. It isn't always rainbows and unicorns, although I wish it were. Reality exists, and life happens. Notice how often you look at the negative aspect of a situation rather than looking at the positive side.

You're not doing anything wrong when you focus on the negative. You're actually responding the way you are biologically wired. Humans react much more to negative news and stories than those of inspiration. There is a reason we can't take our eyes off a train wreck. However, you are no longer a caveman; our survival isn't being threatened. It's time to retrain your brain. When you master seeing the blessing in any situation, no matter how cataclysmic, you have mastered your life.

Just a few years ago, Mike was in one of the darkest places he's ever been. How did his life get this out of control? He began to question everything: who he was, his relationships, his job, and even his family. He wondered if he would ever be happy? Like most people on a spiritual journey, Mike awakened because a health scare gave him no choice. You see, for the past few years, he had been neglecting the signs his body was giving him, not only his physical health, but his mental and emotional health as well.

One particular day during lunch, Mike confided to some of his colleagues that he wasn't feeling right. They knew he was under tremendous stress and could see that he wasn't acting like himself. They insisted Mike see the nurse. His blood pressure was sky high! The nurse told him he needed to call his doctor and make an appointment ASAP.

After running several tests, the doctor did discover that he did have high blood pressure. Thankfully, there wasn't anything more serious. Medication would be necessary, but as for his anxiety and depression, the doctor told Mike he could give him a pill that would treat his symptoms. If he wanted to really heal, though, Mike needed to identify the root cause.

If he was honest with himself, he knew the problem was in his negative mindset.

Overall, Mike had very few reasons to be negative. He had a well-paying career, and his family loved and supported him. Although he wasn't in a romantic relationship, Mike had good friends and an active social life. He'd thought he was happy.

As he began to reflect, Mike recalled that when he was student teaching, his supervisor had accused him of whining and complaining a lot. Later, when he started teaching full-time, several of his colleagues called him out on this, too. He would often feel sorry for himself and would brood over how nothing seemed to ever work out for him. So, guess what? The Universe gave him more of what he didn't actually want. But Mike didn't realize at the time that he was bringing it upon himself.

Then the Universe delivered the cherry on top: Mike became the butt of a very cruel joke. The worst part was that he didn't even know this until several months later, when another colleague finally told him. You can imagine his devastation, learning about the joke, and never knowing this whole time that he was actually the center of it.

This only fueled his anger and negativity, and it made his job even more stressful. He tried to transfer at the end of the school year, but he was denied. He applied for other jobs and didn't get interviewed. It was the proverbial straw that broke the camel's back. Mike refused to continue to work in an environment that was taking years off his life.

That summer, he ran into an old friend who had gone through a pretty significant physical transformation. Mike asked what his friend was doing, and his friend shared that he'd committed to a fitness plan. Although it had reshaped his body, his friend shared that it was the exercise that was changing him from the inside out. His friend was more focused, positive, and emotionally stronger.

Inspired by his friend, that day Mike committed to daily exercise as well. Within a few weeks, he not only noticed how much his body was changing, but how his mindset was shifting, too. The more he exercised, the stronger his body and mind became.

Mike reached out to me and we started working on his spiritual fitness as well. He spent many days at Barnes and Noble reading about the Law of Attraction. As I coached him, using specific processes, his outer reflection became the result of all of the inner work he was doing.

A few months later, Mike was called into his supervisor's office. Surprised, he was offered a job transfer. It was a better offer than the opportunity he was denied earlier. Now, Mike absolutely loves his new environment. His new colleagues value and respect him because he finally appreciates himself. It just goes to prove that the Universe delivers in divine timing, and for our highest good.

Mike is now a poster child for positivity. He uses his social media to inspire others with his daily hashtag #positivity. After all, positivity is contagious!

Speaking of contagious...have you ever had that day where everything just seems to go wrong? You wake up feeling exhausted because you couldn't sleep well. Your alarm didn't go off, so now you're running late. In your half-awakened state, heading to the bathroom, you stub your toe. You can't find your keys; you forget your lunch. Traffic is heavier than usual and you hit every stoplight. Before you know it, you're having a terrible day, and it completely spirals out of control?

All of us experience days like this, myself included. However, learning to pivot to the positive has enabled me to stop the spiral of negativity. As a deliberate creator, I realize that I am consciously crafting my day, so it's up to me to design it the way I want it to go. You have this power too.

Can you be positive all of the time? Absolutely not! That's unrealistic. Some days you just have a freaking lousy day. We all have them. But the faster you recognize your negative speech and thought patterns, the quicker you can flip any situation. This is key! Most of the time I can halt it and choose something different. It takes awareness, time, and practice. Remember, the Universe is responding to your vibration, positivity ranks higher on the emotional scale, which makes you more of a manifesting magnet.

Despite a tumultuous childhood and upbringing, I have always been a very positive person. I have witnessed the universe reward positivity time and time again. The more positive and grateful you are, the more you'll attract more things to be positive and thankful for.

I also learned that it's essential to inventory my environment and the people I spend my time with. Have you ever entered a room when people are complaining and grumbling about something? Most likely, you join the conversation, and within a few minutes, you've become a negative Nelly. Get out of there fast! You don't need the influence of these types of people. As the saying goes, misery loves company. Be aware of the company you keep!

Being an empath, I tend to allow toxic people in my life and space for far too long because I don't want to be unkind or rude. As I am healing, and on this spiritual journey, I have learned that these people are energy vampires, and that it is okay to eliminate them from my life. It's not only okay, but it's also necessary. Let go of toxic people, relationships, and situations. Don't stay entangled in their web of negativity.

Inspired Assignment

Learn to recognize your negative language patterns. Do you gossip and complain about everything, every chance you get? Become aware of how you speak to others and, most importantly, how you speak to yourself. You actually spend more time talking to yourself than others, so become conscious of how you are speaking to yourself. Most people revert to negative self-talk because, again, it is human nature. Awareness of our language patterns serves as a compass to our vibrational frequency. Esther and Jerry Hicks shared a process that can help you learn to pivot your negative thoughts to the positive. This exercise is so simple that it is often underused as a Law of Attraction process. Don't discount its simplicity for its effectiveness.

1. Identify a topic, or area of your life, where you would like to bring in more positive energy or focus. (e.g. money, career, relationships)

2. Now use this starter sentence to answer the question: "Wouldn't it be nice…"

3. For sixty-eight seconds (remember, I taught you the significance of sixty-eight seconds in the Beliefs chapter) rattle off as many answers as you can, starting each one with "wouldn't it be nice." You can also write them down if you prefer a tactile experience. Either way is just as effective. Personally, for this process, I like speaking it aloud because then I can do it basically anywhere and at any time.

   Example:
   Topic: *Toxic work environment*
   Wouldn't it be nice if my colleagues were more helpful to me?
   Wouldn't it be nice if my boss created boundaries?
   Wouldn't it be nice if I had a better relationship with my supervisor?

Wouldn't it be nice if I received a raise?
Wouldn't it be nice if I got promoted?
Wouldn't it be nice if Nicole got transferred?

How does this work? It works because it changes your vibration. When you complain about your toxic work environment, you will continue to attract negative experiences. *Remember, like attracts like.* By using this simple question, you have a different expectation, which allows you to become less resistant. Negative language communicates an unspoken vibration of lack or absence of what you truly desire. It would be most effective if you could immediately pivot to the positive, but most of us cannot. This process is a bridge to get you there.

During the process of writing and editing this chapter, I attended a workshop with Dr. John Demartini. I almost eliminated this chapter, because he spent a good time in his session insisting that what I just wrote about is actually not true. He had conducted a self-study, tracing his negative thoughts for over a year, and reported that he actually did not become more positive. While his workshop was fantastic, and I did have a breakthrough (that was the purpose of the workshop), in this is one area I respectfully disagree with Dr. Demartini. I have never met a curmudgeon who could quickly and easily manifest his or her desires. In fact, most cynical people that I know continuously create more strife, heartache, and lack into their lives. To this day, I have only let go of one client because she refused to address her negativity, and so she did not see results. Every client I have worked with comes with a negativity bias, but as soon as we identify these patterns and release the blocks, abundance flows effortlessly and quickly.

You will have negative thoughts and bad days. You will not be cured of negativity. You are human. However, you now have a tool that allows you to pivot to the positive immediately. The more you do this process, the faster you will pivot, and the quicker you will manifest your desires.

Cavemen had no choice but to be negative; their survival depended on it. You, not so much. Evolution changed our brains to be able to choose positivity. Don't overcomplicate it. It's literally just a decision. Caveman, negative. You, positive.

CHAPTER 20

Authenticity: You Do You, Boo

Authenticity is the daily practice of letting go of who we think we're supposed to be and embracing who we are. ~ Brené Brown

One of my favorite memories of elementary school was our annual Halloween dress-up day. On that day, we were dismissed at lunchtime. My grandfather would pick me up, and my grandmother would have my favorite lunch waiting for me. I'd eat quickly so I could don my Halloween costume and mask; at the time, everyone wore masks. My grandmother would desperately try to secure every piece of my thick red hair under the wig; otherwise, my hair would be a dead giveaway of my identity.

When we returned to school following lunch, the students would file into the classroom silently and sit in a seat that was not our own. The teacher would then come around to each student trying to identify him or her. The goal was to be the last person identified. It took me until sixth grade, but I was finally one of the last students standing.

Halloween provides kids and adults alike the opportunity to try on new identities. I believe Lucy Van Pelt was on to something when she said in *It's the Great Pumpkin, Charlie Brown,* "A person should always choose a costume which is in direct contrast to her own personality." While contemplating authenticity and writing this chapter, this memory immediately popped into my mind because most of us wear masks, disguising our true selves daily, not just on Halloween. We use masks to protect ourselves from others' criticism and judgments. We put on airs so that others accept us. We may even compromise our values at times if it means gaining someone's love and attention. We empower everyone else but ourselves.

Don't get me wrong, sometimes wearing a mask is necessary. We put on different ones at work, home, and socially. Sometimes we have to play the part. If you are speaking to your boss, you probably are not as candid as you may be with your spouse or lover. But if you are continuously hiding behind a mask to avoid showing your true self, it's time to take it off and take a good hard look in the mirror.

Why are you hiding from yourself?

Being authentic doesn't mean you have to hang every piece of dirty laundry on the line or post every painful detail of your life on social media. It means knowing who you are and being unapologetically confident about it. It's the foundation of forming vulnerable and genuine relationships.

Most of the clients I work with struggle with authenticity. Once we begin to delve into their past, unearthing the stories and limiting beliefs, they realize that none of those stories are their own. They have learned this behavior, like we all do, from our well-meaning parents, family, and friends, and have adopted the story and belief as their own. Take my client Nancy for example (her name is changed for privacy).

Nancy began working with me because she was questioning her life's purpose. For over two decades, she had worked in corporate America. To receive a promotion, Nancy worked at least seventy hours a week, did whatever her supervisors told her to do (even when there were some ethical issues), and sacrificed everything, including her health, to get to her goal. Unfortunately—or so she thought at the time—Nancy didn't get the promotion. It was given to a man, whom she swears did not jump through any of the hoops she did. It was a huge wake-up call that she was not living her purpose. Frustrated and angry, Nancy promptly quit that day, and then freaked out when reality hit home.

She was desperate when she came to me. She had just thrown a six-figure salary out the door and didn't know what to do next. Her husband had recently left her and she was now a single mom. She had no formal coaching training, but had coached many colleagues during her time in her corporate job. And here was the other rub: she had no idea what her coaching niche was, or who her ideal client would be, so she decided that she would become a business coach.

I knew the minute she decided this would be her focus, that it was not, in fact, who she was supposed to be. Nancy was resorting to what she knew and what was comfortable. It was what she felt she *should* be, rather than being who she *wanted* to be. Helping clients to identify their passions and purpose is my niche, but for weeks, she resisted my expertise.

During our coaching sessions, I learned a lot about the real Nancy. While she was extremely logical and meticulous with details, she had awakened to her spirituality. For the past year, she had been reading about the Law of Attraction and attending local workshops and classes online. Once, when she was having health issues, a friend suggested she try reiki, and after one session, she was hooked. Nancy found a local reiki master and got certified. She loved helping people. Her former colleagues often sought her out for advice or just to vent. Nancy's light was evident to everyone but herself.

Her husband and friends had begun to notice these changes and they didn't approve. Fearful of their judgment and criticism, she hid that side of herself and threw herself back into a job where she felt undervalued and unappreciated. Simmering below the surface, anger and resentment brewed, because Nancy couldn't be the person she wanted to be.

It was during one of her sessions, that she had a complete breakdown. Nancy confessed that I had been right all along. She was *not* a business coach; she did not want to coach burnt out corporate women like herself. She had left corporate America because it was not her purpose. It had become crystal clear to her that she was a healer in hiding. Using Reiki, EFT (Emotional Freedom Technique, or otherwise known as 'tapping'), and other similar modalities, Nancy had been secretly learning. She decided that what she wanted to do was to help women heal physically, emotionally, and spiritually. Almost instantaneously, all of the pieces of the puzzle came together. By the end of our coaching sessions, she had attracted her first three clients, exceeding her personal goal. One of her clients wrote in a testimonial that Nancy's greatest strength was her "authenticity and vulnerability." When Nancy allowed herself to be authentic, she empowered her clients to do the same.

It is not easy to be our authentic selves, but it is necessary for the manifestation process. Nancy reminded me of this, but I learned it myself the hard way. I am a recovering people-pleaser. For decades, I nearly killed myself to make sure everyone else was happy. I didn't have boundaries, and I allowed others' beliefs, needs, and judgments to dictate my life, which was spinning out of control. So, I resorted to a coping mechanism that I believed had once allowed me options. I began to binge and purge, not just my food, but every feeling that I couldn't stomach (pun intended). My eating disorder raised its ugly head again when I turned thirty years old.

That part of me had laid dormant for almost ten years. But the Universe does this thing where it will repeat lessons until we master them. One afternoon, I went into the bathroom and forgot to lock the door. I had turned on the water to hide the noise, but my youngest daughter walked in and asked, "Mommy, why you throw up?" I was embarrassed, ashamed, and angry that she saw me this way. I was trying to purge away the beliefs and expectations that everyone had of me instead of expressing myself in a healthy and authentic way.

My daughter saved me that day. I immediately found a therapist who specialized in eating disorders and began unpacking decades of trauma. Session after session, I allowed layers of the onion to be peeled back until I was fully exposed. While terrifying, it was actually freeing to let myself to come out from hiding and truly be myself. No one's opinions or judgments would ever prevent me again from marching to the beat of my own drum.

Inspired Assignment

Revealing your true self doesn't have to be scary. It also doesn't have to be all or nothing. Taking small steps in reclaiming your true identity puts you back into alignment with Source. In your journal, explore the following questions.

1. Identify Your Core Values:

   - Who are you at the core?
   - What are your values and beliefs?
   - What ultimately makes you happy?

Do not write what you *think* you should be; write what you *want* and what you truly believe.

2. Awareness and Perception:
   Think objectively and reflect on a time when you were being fake or disingenuous. Why did you feel you couldn't be yourself? What were the emotions you felt? Reflecting on the situation, was it necessary for you to be fake, or could you have been safe to be yourself? Sometimes we have to wear masks for our jobs or life situations, so if you genuinely felt you needed to do that, it's ok. There's no judgment, but I want you to examine it now from a bird's eye view.

3. Speak Your Truth:
   Identify a situation where you haven't been able to communicate your true feelings. It's time to share and speak up for what you need and want. Lordy, my throat chakra has been so blocked for so long, and now I must be careful the filter goes back on occasionally.

Next time you choose your Halloween costume, ask yourself why you selected that particular character or identity. What are the qualities or characteristics it embodies that you wish you possess? Sure, dressing up as Wonder Woman, Superman, or a sexy nurse is fun. But if you are selecting that identity because you want to feel empowered, secure, or sexy, I'm telling you this: *you are already all of those qualities.* Take off the mask and cape and live in the costume you were born in.

CHAPTER 21

Authenticity 2.0

Be yourself; everyone else is already taken. ~ Oscar Wilde

I could write an entire book on authenticity, but for the sake of this one, I will just devote another chapter. It's too important of a topic to gloss over, especially when it comes to manifesting. Also, every time I write another chapter, the Universe gives me a lesson to practice what I preach, and lately, it's all about being one hundred percent real.

Shakespeare wrote, "This above all to thy own self is true." The first thing you need to do is be true to yourself. If you can't be honest with yourself, how the hell can you be honest with anyone else? You may be able to fool others, honey, but you can't fool yourself. Stop trying. It's time to take a look under the hood and see what is really going on.

You may wonder why authenticity matters so much when it comes to manifesting. An astute reader would question me and say, "Wait a minute; hold on, Kelly. Several times you taught us to act as if, pretend, imagine, and visualize what you want. That's not authentic to pretend we have something we don't."

I would say you're correct—partially. The difference is that when you act as if you have the desire already, you put yourself into a vibrational match for your desire. Like attracts like. However, when you are being fake, disingenuous, and not your authentic self, your vibrational frequency matches that low vibration. In other words, because like attracts like, you're only going to attract more low vibrations.

If you refer back to the emotional guidance scale, you will be quickly reminded of how detrimental it is to *not* be your true self. Unless that is what you want, then go for it. If it isn't, you need to take off the mask and stop hiding from who you truly are. The masks can cover you up, but your vibration will always tattle on you.

I was a star when I was a little girl. Literally. I stood with my jar, a rag, and a star cutout attached to my face, awaiting the judge's evaluation. I recited the poem *Somebody Has To*, by Shel Silverstein, and won the annual storytelling contest. My picture appeared in the local newspaper with a little blurb. It was my first fifteen minutes of fame, and like that star, I wasn't afraid to shine.

Growing up in the inner city, I spent my childhood summers at a playground that was steps away from my grandparents' house. The neighbourhood summer program ran all day on Monday through Friday, with occasional special evening activities. It was free, which was a gift to so many parents like mine, who didn't have the extra money to join the local pool or enroll us in expensive summer camps. Each playground employed two leaders who organized sports, crafts, and theater games each day. There was an annual talent show, musical theater performance, contests, and a lantern parade. One of the leaders encouraged me to enter the storytelling contest that I won. I didn't realize it until now, but that contest planted the seeds; I still love storytelling.

I wasn't afraid to be myself as a child. I loved singing, dancing, and acting. Like many little girls, my mom put me in dance and gymnastics classes. I signed up for the annual talent shows at the playground and throughout elementary school. In middle school, I landed roles in all of the plays. I loved to perform and didn't care about the haters—until I eventually did.

Like most adolescents, I began to mold myself into the latest trends and fads. If my best friend was doing it, so was I. I had to buy clothes from Gap and Express because that's where the rich, popular kids shopped, even though I really didn't like the style. Beaten down by my friends, parents, and societal expectations of who and what I was supposed to be, I decided it wasn't safe to be Kelly.

While I held tight to my morals and convictions, I let go of my own interests to appease everyone else. I had an ex-boyfriend who went totally hippie. In every effort to get back together with him, I went out and bought a green pair of chucks, a hippie-style shirt, and fringed jean shorts. This was an outfit that I would never typically wear, but I was desperate to conform to what I believed he wanted. Over the years, the constant judgment and criticism stole this once confident, free-spirited, redhead. It made her into someone who worried about what everyone thought about her.

You would think that after getting married and having children, I would totally accept myself, but that wasn't the case. I felt I had to wear different masks at work, at home, and in public. I would morph like a chameleon to whomever was in front of me. While my husband and kids got to see the raw, flawed me, I tried to display the perfect mother-wife-teacher facade for everyone else. Many days, I would cry, feeling like most women do, a complete failure and a fraud. Society sets unrealistic standards and rules that most humans, especially those of us raising them, could never meet.

While I love social media, it truly doesn't help. The facade's that most people put on are massive. The pictures and posts are not a true reflection of how they genuinely live all of the time. I'm guilty of this, but I don't believe that makes me less authentic or genuine. Mainly, it's because my family doesn't want to hang our dirty laundry for all the world to see. I do get that, and I don't think it is necessary to expose your vulnerabilities. As long as your actions match your words and values, then you know you are practicing authenticity.

Who are you when others are watching? Have you ever heard the story of meeting or seeing a celebrity you fangirl (or fanboy) in public? You think this person is always patient, kind, and sweet. Then she snaps at her waiter and you realize this is not the person you believed her to be. She's scolding him, complaining incessantly. There is an expression about character that goes something like: how people treat waiters, airline attendants, and service workers actually shows their true colors. Reflect on yourself. How do you behave in these situations? It may be painful to look at yourself under the microscope, but the Universe knows your true colors.

Because when you think you're faking it until you are making it, your vibration is telling a whole different story. You need to get honest with yourself and really delve into who you are when no one else is watching.

When you are authentic, you give others permission to be authentic. Don't dim your light and hide. The stars don't stop shining when one burns out. They each shine as brightly as they can. As a result, we have a beautifully lit sky.

Inspired Assignment

I began working with both a traditional therapist and an energy healer. The role of my therapist is to help me delve into old wounds that have resurfaced, and my energy healer is, well, healing them. My healer introduced me to the following exercise, and I am not going to lie...OMG, it is difficult and painful, but after only one week, I could honestly say, "holy moly, it's working!" You will need a mirror, your journal, and time set aside both in the morning and evening.

1. In the morning after waking, and before you go to bed, sit or stand in front of a mirror. If you don't have a full-length mirror, a hand-held mirror is fine. Set a timer for one minute (this seemed like an eternity the first few times) and just gaze into your own eyes. Really look deep into your eyes; they are the portal to your soul. Allow whatever emotion rises up to come. Don't hold back tears, laughter, or crying. Just allow any and all of the feelings to flood over you without judgment.

2. Now, using the words, *I am*, create three affirmations that are true—and positive—about yourself. The affirmations that my healer created with me are:

   I am *beautiful*
   I am *love*
   I am *free will*

3. Say these affirmations three times as you continue to gaze into your eyes.

4. Take a few minutes each time to journal about your experience. What emotions came up? How are you feeling? There's no "wrong" thing to write, so just free write.

5. Repeat this process before bedtime.

6. Try it for seven days. If you miss a day, you will need to start over on day one. Consistency is key. I had to restart three times!

The first day I tried this, I looked at myself in the mirror and completely broke down sobbing. I sincerely couldn't look into my own eyes. I called my healer in hysterics. She's a straight shooter and told me to "hang up and get my arse in front of the mirror and do it again." I complied, but cried hysterically for the entire minute.

The same thing happened when I repeated the exercise at bedtime. In my journal, I wrote about how painful it was to look into my own eyes, because I felt like I had severely abused the little girl that I caught a glimpse of in those first few seconds. I carried on, though, and each day became easier, and I began to believe the affirmations. My true self began to emerge as I allowed the walls to come down. My therapist even noticed, commenting that "my eyes looked different."

So, you may be wondering what this inspired assignment has to do with authenticity? Mirror work (also written about by Louise Hay) enables us to see our true selves. We use mirrors to see how we look on the outside, but they also serve as a tool to see who we indeed are inside. If you are willing to spend the time looking beyond the looking glass, you will catch a glimpse of who you are when you come into the world naked...totally and authentically *you*!

Somebody Has To

Somebody has to go polish the stars,
They're looking a little bit dull.
Somebody has to go polish the stars,
For the eagles and starlings and gulls
Have all been complaining they're tarnished and worn,
They say they want new ones we cannot afford.
So please get your rags
And your polishing jars,
Somebody has to go polish the stars.

~ Shel Silverstein, A Light in the Attic

CHAPTER 22

Forgiveness

Forgiveness is a gift you give yourself. ~ Suzanne Somers

When I was in college, I served as the President of the Pledge of Integrity committee. While we didn't implement a strict honor code, it was the expectation that every student would voluntarily sign the pledge and promise to uphold the value of integrity. One of our tasks was to teach the Freshman class about academic dishonesty, plagiarism, and cheating. Not an exciting or easy topic to engage college-aged students. I proposed that we write, produce, and perform a skit.

The stage was set. The setting was inside a grocery store; a long table served as the checkout line. My role was the cashier. The other committee members were shoppers who brought various items to me to be scanned. The problem was that the items they brought to me didn't have prices, so I would very loudly have to yell out, "price check on condoms," or "price check on tampons." Our goal was to get the audience to pay attention and we thought some humor would help. It did. After calling out several tangible items, other committee members tried to scan their items: integrity, morality, love. When they got to me, and I asked for a price check on these items, there was silence. How much does integrity cost? Morality? Love? The point of the skit was that you can't assign a price to something so priceless.

Forgiveness is one of these invaluable gifts. One cannot put a price tag on forgiveness, yet it can cost us our lives if we can't forgive. Many people are imprisoned in their past because they cannot forgive someone who hurt them. The fact is, we are human, which means we are fallible. We have all needed forgiveness at some point in our lives. Sometimes we are the victim, but other times we were the perpetrator.

There are many things that forgiveness is *not*. Forgiveness is not forgetting. When we forgive someone who has wronged us, we are not condoning their behavior. Forgiveness is not forgetting the pain we have endured. It's not pretending that the action didn't take place. It's not denying the genuine emotions we felt as a result of the transgression. In fact, forgiveness is activated when we give voice to our pain.

Forgiveness is not weakness, either. In fact, I think the ability to forgive is one of the greatest strengths that you can possess. It takes a powerful person to forgive someone unconditionally.

Forgiveness is not always easy. It takes time and deliberate intention. Usually, it's complicated and overwhelming. It may seem impossible to forgive someone when you may never receive any sign of remorse or apology.

Why is forgiveness so important? As vibrational beings, we are continually sending out a frequency. If we are not forgiving, we are not vibrating at the highest levels. We become stuck in the levels of anger and resentment, which bind us to lower vibrations. We become trapped and imprisoned in our own emotions. Forgiveness is the key to freedom.

If we don't forgive others or ourselves, we emit a frequency that doesn't match our desires. Forgiving is not forgetting; it is letting go, so that we can heal.

I learned about forgiveness from my father. My father is a recovering alcoholic and drug addict. His drug of choice was cocaine. Like most people fighting addictions, he used drugs to numb the pain of his childhood. At the age of eighteen, he and my mom found themselves parents and they got married because, back then, it was the "right thing to do." My father didn't want me. He was still a child himself. After less than two years, he and my mom divorced, and she took full custody of me. My father was granted visitation, though.

During my childhood, my dad was in and out of my life. Because it was sporadic, I thought it was normal. One day, I was at the playground when my mom called me home. She said my dad had just called and wanted to see me. It was my choice if I wanted to go. I remember that day clearly and said, "Sure!" I was about eight years old, and to me, it didn't matter that I hadn't seen him in years.

A week later, dad picked me up, and we went to dinner and played cards at his house. From that point on, the visits were pretty consistent and regular for a while. During that time, my dad didn't have a driver's license, so he would walk me to his house—he only lived a few blocks away—where he would shower, we'd eat dinner that he'd picked up from a local place, and we would play cards or games. I enjoyed those times with my dad until the day I peeked into the shoebox.

My dad had a shoebox underneath his stereo equipment. I noticed it each time I went, but my dad never seemed to have a new pair of shoes. One day while he was showering, my curiosity got the best of me, and I opened the box. I gasped, and my heart sank. The secret shoebox contained drug paraphernalia, pot, and residue of cocaine. Although I was only in fourth grade, I somehow knew those items were associated with drugs. That is how I discovered my father was a drug addict.

I didn't tell my mother; I didn't tell anyone. That fear is still palpable even as I recall that moment. Fortunately, the Universe intervened, As my dad used more and more, he slipped out of my life again. I was secretly grateful because I was terrified to be around him. Year after year passed. My ninth-grade prom (and first boyfriend) came and went, dances, football games (I was a cheerleader), and my confirmation, along with another million small moments that he missed. I was angry, hurt, and resentful. How dare my father choose drugs over his only daughter, his only child, for that matter?

When I was sixteen, after three relapses and rehab, my father finally got sober. During that time, I made an effort to learn about his disease. I went to therapy and AL Anon meetings. It has taken decades, but together we both healed childhood trauma, and we have forgiven each other.

My father celebrated his twenty-ninth year of sobriety in 2021. Our relationship is stronger now than ever. Forgiveness was the long, winding path that allowed us to reconcile our fractured relationship. I came to understand that my father deserves forgiveness because he, like me, is a child of God/Source/Spirit. When we don't forgive, we separate ourselves from our divinity. It is my belief that we are all one, so by not forgiving him, I would not forgive myself.

When we moved to Hawai'i, I was introduced to the sacred forgiveness practice of *Ho'oponopono*. While I didn't know about it when I faced the decision to forgive my father, I have come to understand *Ho'oponopono*; we are always both part of the solution and problem. My dad's addiction was not just his issue. It was mine, his parents, their parents, and every ancestor. While I may have disagreed before coming to understand that, I played a part in my father's addiction. Though, I didn't do the drugs, I now understand my role.

I am not a trained expert, so please only use this process for yourself. It is a sacred Hawaiian practice and needs to be treated as such. However, even at the primary level, I have found it to be a powerful practice for forgiveness.

Inspired Assignment

1. Think of the person you want to forgive.

2. Imagine this person standing in front of you. Visualize looking at him or her deeply in the eye. This may be difficult, but I feel when I do this for myself, I begin to feel more empathy and compassion because I'm reminded that as a spiritual being, we are all one; there is no separation. Our physical bodies merely house our souls, which are connected. If I am him, and he is me, I realize forgiveness is essential to allow myself freedom.

3. Say the following phrases aloud:

   > *I'm sorry*
   > *Please forgive me*
   > *Thank you*
   > *I love you*

4. I practice this when I awake, and before I go to sleep. How often I use this practice depends on whom I have to forgive. It took me years to forgive my father, so it may take you the same, or longer. The hope is that you now have a tool to help you forgive faster.

These phrases may evoke a lot of emotion. Initially, you may say them with anger or resentment. That's okay; say them anyway. Eventually, your tone softens. Your heart becomes more open, and forgiveness will replace those bitter feelings. I've practiced it on a few people whom I've needed to forgive, and I can assure you they were people who may not seem worthy of forgiveness. But it's not about them. It's about me.

I've received many gifts over my lifetime from loved ones. Many of which I don't even remember. But there's one gift that I cherish to this day. It's invaluable. It wasn't wrapped in fancy paper or tied with a pretty bow. It actually was a gift I gave myself. It was the day I forgave my father and set myself free.

CHAPTER 23

Attitude of Gratitude

Gratitude turns what we have into enough. ~ Anonymous

What if I told you I have the *key* secret to manifesting? It is free, available to anyone, and if used daily, can make you a manifesting magnet. The secret is practicing gratitude. Gratitude is accessible to everyone. It does not discriminate based on race, gender, or sexuality. Think of the manifestation steps I outlined as the ingredients, and gratitude is the perfect bowl in which to mix them all together.

As explained by Abraham in the book, "*Ask and It Is Given: Learning to Manifest Your Desires,*" the emotional guidance scale is a spectrum of our feelings and emotions, in sequence from our highest vibrational feelings to our lowest.

As Abraham explains, to raise your vibration, it is easier to take a small step from one emotion to the next rather than trying to leap to the top of the scale. However, I challenge this statement, because I do believe that gratitude can get us to the top relatively quickly. Every human being, no matter how low they are on the scale, if they practice gratitude, can make significant life-changing transformations in a much shorter time.

On the vibrational scale, gratitude is an emotion next to love. Love is the highest vibration, and gratitude is pretty much second. Remember, you are like a radio. Each day you send out a frequency. If your vibration aligns with the same frequency of your desire, you will attract what you want. Gratitude allows you to tune into the highest frequencies easier and faster than if you are vibrating in despair, lack, or depression.

Gratitude is not reserved just for material items. It encompasses your entire being. You can, and should, be grateful for your family, friends, health, love, and so on. Practicing gratitude has a snowball effect. The more you align yourself to its frequency, the more things will show up for which you will be thankful.

In August 2017, I was invited by a local friend to join a gratitude group on Facebook. Yes, I know—who the heck still uses Facebook? —but bear with me. The group is called "100 Days of Gratitude—All Unicorns Welcome." The purpose of the group is simple: challenge and commit yourself to post anything for which you are grateful every day for one hundred days. Why unicorns? The founder, Shannon, believes we all have a little unicorn within us. I was intrigued by the title of the group and I am always up for a challenge.

It also reminded me of a book I had read several years ago, when I still lived in Pennsylvania, entitled *365 Thank You's: The Year a Simple Act of Daily Gratitude Changed My Life* by John Kralik. Every day, for three hundred and sixty-five days, John wrote a thank you letter for acts of kindness or gifts that he received throughout his life from various people, such as coworkers, enemies, school friends, doctors, and anyone who had done something good for him. It only took a few notes for surprising benefits to flow into his life, and by the end of the year, his life completely transformed. If John could be that profoundly changed, could I experience the same kind of transformation?

I still didn't dive in. Honestly, I stalked the group for several weeks, checking out what everybody else was posting. There was a part of me that was afraid to commit. One hundred days seemed like a very long time.

Finally, on September 1, 2017, I posted my first gratitude list. Within minutes, I had several likes and several comments from the members welcoming me to the group and introducing themselves. The seed was planted, but never could I have imagined the flower that was about to bloom. Being a very goal-oriented person, I really wanted to make sure that I made it to one hundred days, so I mapped it out in my planner and set the alarm on my phone. I didn't want to miss a day. Over the next hundred days, I met a lot of people in the group. I learned about their families, where they worked, and if they had children. I found out what their favorite foods were and what they did for fun on weekends. They became my friends, and I really looked forward to reading their lists each day. As each person reached their hundredth day, we weren't ready to leave this sacred community, so many of us decided to go for a whole year and some of us, like me, beyond.

One day, a woman posted that she really had nothing to be grateful for. But she didn't want to miss a day, and she apologized that her post may sound negative. She simply wanted some positive vibes and prayers. Her toilet had clogged, and she literally had—well, you know—that stuff floating around, which caused her ceiling to leak, and the floor was damaged. For what could she possibly be grateful?

One thing this practice has taught me is to pivot to the positive. Even in the seemingly worst situations, you always have a choice. You can react negatively, or pivot to an attitude of gratitude.

I commented on her post and suggested she pivot this. "You have a toilet," I observed, "which means you have a home. It was flushing before it broke, so you must have electricity and water, which means you have money to pay for the house and those bills." Many people who are living in third world countries, would die for a running toilet (even a flooded one), or a glass of freshwater. So, even though her day was crappy (literally and figuratively), she was able to pivot a stinky (pun intended) situation into a positive one. Little did I know that in only a few days, I would need to take my own advice.

I was chaperoning our school's annual senior camp trip when I got the devastating news. My friend, Wanda, passed away suddenly. I had met Wanda in the gratitude group. I had never met her in real life, as she lived on the mainland, but I didn't have to physically meet her to know her. Wanda loved her family, her cat, plants, workouts, and delicious meals. Her responses to members of the gratitude group were detailed and authentic. She painted with words and I was always honored when she responded to one of mine. She always wrote, "thanks doll," when I responded to hers.

Her posts told a story of a woman who didn't just talk about gratitude, she lived it in her speech and in her daily actions and interactions.

Wanda was scheduled for surgery, so on October eighteenth of that year, she sent a quick note to the group. It was the last post she would ever write:

Good morning Guys and Dolls! Grateful to be alive and hoping to stay that way. Going in for surgery. My daughter or I will update post-op. Always remain grateful and joyous!

At that moment, I was so grateful for my spirituality. I can't help but believe that God, spirit, Source (whatever you may believe in), used Wanda as an instrument to teach us the *true* meaning of gratitude. Her passing was a reminder that giving thanks should not be reserved just for Thanksgiving Day, or when you feel obligated to write a thank you card for a birthday gift. As cliche as it sounds, Wanda's attitude of gratitude reminds us that we should be thankful for every day we wake up; we are not promised tomorrow.

Wanda's post changed my life and reaffirmed how sacred and essential this practice is. It costs nothing but my time, but the rewards are invaluable. It has truly transformed my life in several significant ways. Although a usually positive person, it has made me much more positive, even in the worst situations. As a result, I can pivot negative thoughts much more quickly. Remember, thoughts become things, so if you are continually emitting negative thoughts, you'll get negativity. By expressing gratitude for what I have, or the things that come into my life, I manifest more things to be grateful for.

The Winter of 2019 was one of the most challenging times in my family's lives. My cousin, and one of my husband's closest friends, died within about one month of each other due to cancer. Both were diagnosed barely five months before their passing. They were only forty-one years old, and left behind a toddler and two young girls. These two vibrant, once seemingly healthy people, were living their best lives with beautiful families, homes, and skyrocketing careers. How was this fair? Why them? They were generous, loving, and spiritual people, who gave unconditionally to their families, friends, and communities. It wasn't fair. I could have stayed in that negative space, shaken my fist at God, and wallowed in angry grief, or

I could be grateful for the years I had with each of them, for the memories we shared and created, and for the beautiful children they have that will become their legacies.

Years ago, before writing out my gratitude every single day, these tragic losses would have spiraled me into a terrible place, but gratitude has allowed me to move past grief to truly celebrate their lives. Knowing both of them so profoundly, that is exactly what they would have wanted. Don't misread this. You need to grieve; you need to feel it to heal it. Their deaths impacted me significantly, but my gratitude practice reminded me that there is always, always something to be grateful for.

Inspired Assignment

So, now I challenge you! Get a journal, notebook, or piece of paper, and something to write with. Commit to writing three to five gratitude statements every day for the next thirty days. If it seems like there is nothing for which to be grateful on a given day, look around your environment. Try to focus on different things each day, but if you repeat something, that's totally fine. I know you will find something.

Research shows that we create a new habit in about twenty-one days, so give yourself the time and space to do this. It will only take about five minutes each day. Set a reminder on your phone or an alarm clock. Pick a time of day that works best for you; anytime that works for you is the best time! Some people like to begin their day with gratitude. I chose to write mine every night before I go to bed. I do encourage you to write each day. Some people like to verbally express them aloud, but I believe the pen is mightier than the sword. If you miss a day, just write when you remember.

After the thirty days, take a moment and reflect on how this practice is changing your life. Have you received unexpected gifts, notes, or compliments? How has your attitude changed? Will you continue this practice for thirty more days or longer? Honestly, there is no wrong way to practice gratitude. In the words of the Nike motto: *Just do it!*

Practicing gratitude should be part of your daily habit, just like brushing your teeth. Gratitude turns what we have into enough. It is the flashlight that illuminates the darkest paths. May Wanda's last words inspire you to "always remain grateful and joyous!"

CHAPTER 24

What's Next?

You don't have to see the whole staircase, just take the first step.
~ Martin Luther King, Jr.

Congratulations! You've made it! You now have the steps and tools to become the deliberate creator you have always been. Not only have we covered the five steps of my manifesting process, but many topics that will help you align yourself to the vibrational frequency of your desires. Although it may have been an "easy read" (that was my intention, by the way), the goal was to launch you on a journey of self-discovery and awakening.

The joy is in the journey. When we finally reach our destination, we rarely stay there long. The steps in this process are meant to be a rinse-and-repeat. I encourage you to go back and reread specific chapters when you need reminders. Revisit the inspired assignments as often as you need. Your work is not finished; it's actually just begun!

How this book evolved is a manifestation in itself. In the summer of 2016, I traveled with my thirteen-year-old daughter to New York City, so she could attend a prestigious theater camp. Pennsylvania was my home for thirty-eight years, so it was fun to be back on the East Coast to visit our family and friends.

One of those friends, Jay, had introduced me to *The Secret* in 2009, and my spiritual journey began. That same friend wanted to catch up on our move to Hawai'i, so we headed up to her Uptown apartment for lunch, playtime, and conversation. Although a year had passed since we'd seen each other, it was as if we hadn't missed a single hour apart. Of course, our conversation centered around the Law of Attraction, and what we both had manifested in our lives. I mentioned to her that two psychics have told me I would write books. One challenged me flat out, "Why haven't you written a book? The world needs to hear what you have to say." I don't know about that, but I guess this book will determine if he's correct. By the way, everything else he told me has come true!

Jay asked me a similar question: why haven't you written a book? Honestly, I wasn't sure what I was supposed to write about. We discussed a few ideas, and she finally suggested I just start writing. I love to write, but for some reason, every time I sat down to type, nothing appeared on the page. Of course, she suggested meditation, and it was still something I was just dabbling in, but I couldn't quiet my mind.

We finished lunch, exchanged hugs all around, and then my daughter and I got back on the subway to head to Chelsea's Pier (that's another manifestation story for another time) where we spent the afternoon bowling. While we enjoyed a drink and bowled miserably (we even used the bumpers), Jay texted to tell me she just had a vision of herself sitting on a beach, reading my book entitled Five Steps to… by Kelly Weaver, but she couldn't see any more of the title.

That's not the end of the story. I thought about her text and that title for the rest of our days in New York City, but nothing else came to me. Although I now had a partial title, I still had no real idea of actual content. Nothing. Finally, after a life-changing experience for my daughter, and a heart and soul filling trip for both of us, it was time to head back to Hawai'i. But it was another spiritual intervention that would breathe life into my book.

It was during that same timeframe that I had also begun the year-long Quantum Success Coaching Academy life coaching program that I was taking to become a certified Law of Attraction Coach. In our first class, we had closed with a beautiful meditation. We were asked to envision ourselves one year from that date and to give our future selves a gift. It could be anything, tangible or intangible. The gift I had given myself was a book that I had written.

Months passed, and from time to time, I would look at my idea. Many times, I tried to sit down and force myself to write; after all, I now had a title and a crude outline. Nothing. Not a single word fell onto the page.

On February 1, 2017, I committed to walking or exercising for one hundred days, and to blog about the transformations I may have physically and spiritually. During one of those walks, the entire book downloaded into my brain. Spirit whispered, "Use the word *aloha* as an acronym to teach people how to manifest their dream lives." Somewhere in that message, I was also guided to research the true meaning of aloha, because it was the key to the entire book. As soon as I got home, I opened a new Google doc and eagerly sat down to type.... But still the words refused to flow.

I have tried for a few years to write this book. I even had several days alone in Maui, where I promised myself, I would spend every minute writing, while I was cat-sitting for a friend. No husband. No kids. It should have been perfect. I think I wrote a few sentences. Writing a book seemed like it would be easy. After all, I was an English major. I taught teens how to write; I loved writing for pleasure. OMG! How naive, and my sincerest apologies to all writers! What was my problem?!

A year later, I began coaching for Vanessa Simpkins. Vanessa has written and published a few books. Suddenly, it dawned on me to ask her for advice. She suggested I hire her book coach, Les. What the heck was a book coach, I wondered? I soon learned that a book coach is someone who helps a writer identify content, gain clarity, and develop the outline of their book. That was exactly what I needed.

During our first meeting, I knew he was the one who would help me make this dream become a reality. Les was patient with me as I went back and forth about investing in his services. I laugh at myself when I realize that the Universe keeps making me walk my talk. Remember the chapter on decision making?

I signed with Les, and the rest is history.

Well, sort of. Next, I would need a publisher. I was convinced that my book wouldn't be successful if not published by a certain well-known publishing company. But the more I spoke with their representatives, I began to realize it was not a good fit. I had also wanted a particular editor that was unavailable, and I was sure it was a sign to throw in the towel. Finally, in frustration, I spoke up during one of my sessions with my book coach. Les laughed and asked why I hadn't asked sooner. He recommended using Friesen Press and to connect with Emily. Within five minutes of speaking with her, I knew the Universe had orchestrated our meeting! It wasn't until I finally followed my own steps and advice, that everything flowed effortlessly and easily.

The book you hold in your hands is proof that my steps work when you follow them. I set my intention to write this book in 2016. I put in my order and waited patiently for over *five years* for the Universe to bring me the people, the resources, and experience I needed to complete it. And now, here it is in your hands.

I took action. I talked with people who, in turn, introduced me to other people who could help me. I was open to finding a different publisher and editor. I trusted in Divine timing and didn't give up on my dreams. Notice, my initial actions were small. You don't need to do a monumental task all at once. You just need to take one step, then another, then another. When you do, the Universe will show you the whole staircase.

Sometimes it will seem like you take two steps back only to move forward one. Trust that the Universe is leading—or redirecting—you on the path of your highest good. There's a reason I was redirected and not given what I thought I wanted and needed. Even though I don't know why, and I may never know, I allowed my faith to be greater than my fear. Allow the Universe to take the wheel and stop looking in the rearview mirror.

When I let go of how I would find a publisher and editor, the Universe placed people in my path to help me. For months, whenever I tried to manipulate the outcome, my resistance only put me in more opposition. When I allowed the Universe to work, and let go of any expectations, the Universe delivered what I needed right on time. Not one minute sooner or later.

I behaved as if I had already written the book. When I gave myself that book during my meditation, I visualized the cover. I saw my name as the author. As I held it in my hands, emotions flooded me like a wave. I stood confidently, beaming in pride, as I looked down on years of accomplishment.

Reflect on these song lyrics of my ultimate favorite song, "A Million Dreams" from the movie, *The Greatest Showman.* If you have not watched this movie, I'm assigning you to do so. This movie is all about deliberate creation and what can happen when you forget to include love as the container.

They can say, they can say it all sounds crazy
They can say, they can say we've lost our minds
I don't care, I don't care if they call us crazy
Runaway to a world that we design
Every night I lie in bed
The brightest colors fill my head
A million dreams are keeping me awake
I think of what the world could be
A vision of the one I see
A million dreams is all it's gonna take
A million dreams for the world we're gonna make...

Inspired Assignment

Throughout the book, I have covered many topics and taught you how to become a Master Manifestor. The key is to be in vibrational alignment with your intention. Let's review the five steps in my process to manifest your dreams:

A is for Ask:

Be clear and specific when you ask for your desire. The Universe likes details. Do you remember the three keys for asking: clarity, vibration and belief?

1. Visualize using all five senses and be crystal clear on your desire.

2. Be aware of the vibrations you are emitting; if your thoughts and vibrations are negative, pivot to the positive.

3.   Believe that you will receive it!

L is for Listen:
Every day, the Universe whispers or, in some cases, sounds the alarm to get your attention. Listen with your ears and eyes. Signs are all around you. Don't dismiss 'coincidences' that are, in fact, synchronicities—or what I like to call God nods. Most importantly, listen to your intuition! It's not exclusive to mothers; you have the answer inside you. An excellent method of retraining yourself to stop and reconnect is through meditation. If you're new to meditation, try the *Calm* app, or the *Stop, Breath, & Think Kids* app. Practice patience, and practice watching for the signs. Dial into awareness and ask the Universe to show you your personal message.

O is for Open:
Although you may ask for a brand-new red Jaguar, be open to what the Universe delivers. The Universe knows what is best for us and for our highest good. If a door of opportunity opens, walk in, even if it's not the door you knocked upon. The Universe may give you something that is actually better than what you expected or were looking for. Open your heart, mind, eyes, and ears to what is possible, not merely what you *think* you want.

H is for How:
Letting go of the *how* is a critical step in the manifesting process. It is not up to you to try to orchestrate the outcome; the Universe has a million ways and means that you can't even imagine. By letting go of the outcome, you are surrendering and allowing yourself to receive, and are aligning your vibration to the same frequency of the desire. Remember: the Universe doesn't speak a language; it speaks vibration. If you stress about how your desire will manifest or try to manipulate how it will arrive, you only attract more worry and doubt. The *how* is none of your damn business. Just place your order and allow the Universe's kitchen to cook up your desire. It's on its way in Divine timing.

A is for Act as If:

Visualization is imagining something as if it has already happened, like the golfer who sees his perfect stroke before he even picks up his club. When you dress for and act the part of your desire, it is preparation for the manifestation, aligning you with the frequency of your desire. By acting as if you manifested your wish into a tangible form, you quickly align with the vibrational frequency of gratitude, which allows it to be delivered in Divine timing. Express gratitude and allow yourself to feel every emotion around your desire.

You now have the steps and all the tools you need to live your own aloha! It's time to stop sitting on the sidelines and jump into the game. You get one life—that you remember. Don't you want to live it to the fullest?

When Spirit told me to use the word *aloha* as the steps for my manifestation process, I knew immediately why: *aloha* at its essence and core means *love*. If you want to manifest any desire, it must come from a place of love. Love is the highest vibrational frequency. Are you ready to live your own aloha? What are you waiting for?

BONUS CHAPTER

Work with Kelly

Nothing will work unless you do. ~ Maya Angelou

It's hard to live your life to the fullest when you're stuck, consumed by fear, and when the odds are stacked against you. It's certainly harder when you're not sure what your life's purpose even is…

… moving your family across the state, country, or across the world?

… pursuing your dream career, even if it means quitting your safe and secure job?

… breaking free of a dead-end relationship, believing that your soulmate is waiting for you?

But you are sure of one thing: you know that "this" is not it. You know there's more! And that you are called to become more, to do more, to give more, to achieve more. And you are done with the uncomfortable; you're determined to break free, and break through, all the blocks that are holding you back. You are motivated. It's now or never!

Look, I've been where you are, and then some! My life was anything but sunshine and rainbows. There was plenty of trauma, abuse, neglect, addiction, pain, and fear...

I know how it feels to sit there, with your life flashing before your eyes, and knowing that you have the decision to make: do you continue the way things are? Do you make the decision to make the change? And most importantly, what's the first step? Can you really do this?

I know that there's no "perfect" moment to start. In fact, by the time you *feel* ready, it will already be too late. Life has taught me this the hard way—a broken ankle healed my broken soul.

So, if I did it, I know that you can, too! Only, this time, you're not alone. I'll be right there with you.

Together, we will develop strategies, techniques, step-by-step tangible processes, and practical tools that are one hundred percent customized to your needs and unique learning style, to help you see immediate shifts.

During our time together, you will:

- Gain clarity on your life's purpose, so that you can live a life full of passion
- Use Law of Attraction processes to manifest your desires
- Identify and remove even the most deeply-rooted blocks that are keeping you from abundance
- Dissolve fears that are keeping you paralyzed and going in circles
- Take inspired action every day for the rest of your life
- Shatter your limits, no matter how big or small

As a Law of Attraction coach, I work one-on-one with clients from all over the world, using Law of Attraction processes, to help them manifest careers, relationships, money, homes, or whatever they desire. . . If you have the internet, a computer, and a dream, let's work together to manifest the life you were born to live!

Hawaiians never say good-bye. It's time to say *a hui hou* (until we meet again).

Let's Connect

Check out my website Soulvivor808.com to book a **FREE** 30-minute clarity call with me!

Email me at www.Soulvivor808@gmail.com
Find me on Facebook @Manifesting Miracles
Instagram: soulvivor808
Twitter: @soulvivor808
LinkedIn: www.linkedin.com/in/soulvivor808

Need a keynote speaker to inspire and motivate your conference, retreat, or group? Email me for more information regarding speaking engagements.

Are you interested in attending a retreat on Oahu? Connect with me for available dates and events.

Testimonials

Because of [the tools Kelly gave me], I now experience faster progress in bigger manifestations, greater positivity on a daily basis, greater clarity, and seeing things in different perspectives.

A. Burns, Self Employed

Kelly is a fantastic and honest coach. She is trustworthy and professional at all times. Her advice and messages are always positive and for the benefit of her clients. I am so thrilled with my progress under her watchful eye and heart. I absolutely recommend Kelly as a life coach. She is amazing!!!

Michelle Macias, Teacher

Kelly is a gifted listener, intuitive guide, and coach. Before working with Kelly, I would get lost in my mind with the question of how something was going to unfold. How would I create a new career path?

Stacy Cohen, *Chief of Everything* and *The Art of Freedom*

Kelly was extremely kind, insightful, and inspirational.

Michael Duarte, Teacher

Kelly Weaver taught me to intentionally make my life's movements attractive. Kelly Weaver, you have changed my life.

Stacy Butler, Author of *They Called Me Queen B*

Kelly has helped me see the person I am. She helped me become more confident and see the positive in everyday life. I have become more at peace and happy.

Christine, Self-Employed

Acknowledgments

Writing a book has always been a dream of mine. It began when I learned how to write. In sixth grade, I wrote my first "chapter" book. Unfortunately, it somehow got thrown away over these years. I wrote short stories and poems. One poem was published in some random anthology, and another one of my stories won a contest sponsored by my local newspaper.

In seventh grade, I met Mrs. Carol B. Henrich, and my life changed forever. Although she taught me grammar and how to diagram sentences, those are not the lessons I remember. She taught me about life and what it means to live a life you love. Mrs. Henrich became a mother figure to me at a time in my life when I needed a role model. She showed me that I could combine my love of reading and writing by becoming a teacher. That seed was planted; here I am, an educator of more than twenty-two years, and a published author.

One day, she took me to lunch at Arby's and over a roast beef sandwich and a vanilla milkshake, she told me she had been battling cancer, and it had spread. Mrs. Henrich modeled strength, perseverance, and resilience. When she was diagnosed, she flat out told the doctor, "I'm not going to die because I still have shopping to do." Her positive attitude and sense of humor never wavered.

The last day I saw her was on Mother's Day. She had been unconscious and unresponsive. I had written her a letter and read it to her anyway. When I was finished, she opened her beautiful eyes one last time for me; I knew she heard every word.

During my junior year in high school, she passed away. It was the first significant loss I had ever experienced in my life. That day I made a promise to her mother, June Burkert, that I would be Carol's legacy. I also promised her I would write a book. June is currently ninety-five-years-young, living her own aloha with her boyfriend and bowling in a weekly league. This is for you, June and Carol!

My husband, Scott: Since we met when we were sixteen years old, you know I have carried this dream in my heart. Thank you for carving out space in the garage to give me a quiet place to write. More importantly, thank you for supporting me and loving me, unconditionally.

Sydney Elizabeth & Saige Arden: You are my greatest teachers. You are the reason my heart beats and why I breathe. Until I became a mother, I genuinely don't think I understood what it meant to love someone unconditionally. Thank you for choosing me to be your mom. I am blessed to have such incredible daughters who are going to change this world.

Kaila: I may not have conceived you or birthed you, but the Universe knew I needed another daughter. Watching you grow from a seventh grader into the beautiful woman you are today has been an honor and privilege. I know that life didn't deal you the best hand, but you've played the cards the best way you knew how. I cherish the memories of parties, dinners, shopping for your first prom dress, and tucking you in on those nights you felt scared. Although I lost you for a short while, I thank God he allowed you to come back into our lives. I will always be your, Mim, no matter how old we both get.

Mom: Thank you for choosing me. I know it wasn't easy being so young, and you made a lot of sacrifices for me over the years. You have been the one person in my life who has been my unconditional support and cheerleader. You've supported every goal and dream I have had without question, concern, or criticism. You believed in me when I didn't believe in myself. I love and appreciate you more than I could ever express.

Mike: When I found out mom was pregnant with you, I told everyone who would listen that I was going to be a big sister. I prayed for you for *years*! I could not wait for you to arrive; I still remember getting the call at Nan and Pop's that you were born; it was one of the best days of my life. I know we weren't close over the years because of our age difference, but I always loved having you as my baby brother, and I still do. I love our relationship now and how much it has grown the past few decades. I'm so proud of the hard-working and caring man you have become.

Dad: Our relationship was quite the rollercoaster ride for many years while you were getting sober. You were in my life and then out; however, here we are twenty-eight years later, stronger than ever. Getting sober was the best gift you could have given not only yourself, but for me, too. I'm so proud of you, dad. Here's to twenty-eight more years and beyond.

Ron and Cook: From the first day I met you, you accepted me unconditionally. It didn't matter what side of the tracks I came from or what my family life was like, you saw me, Kelly. You've loved and treated me like your daughter. Over the years, you helped take care of Syd and Saige and create lasting memories with them and me. I am so blessed to have the world's best in-laws!

Mark, my brother-in-law: I've known you since you were a chubby ten-year-old who lived on his rollerblades. You love Disney more than people love their children. But what I love about you is your *huge* heart. I know it seems like life isn't always fair and you've had your share of struggles. I hope this book showed you that, like Disney, you can tap into your imagination to dream up whatever life you want to live.

Megan: Although we are cousins in family terms, you are the little sister I never had but always wanted. Just like biological sisters, we sure have had our ups and downs. But at the end of the day, blood is thicker than water, and we always return to each other. These past years we have both grown and changed in so many ways. I'm so proud of how you consistently show up for yourself and take radical responsibility. It's not easy to look at ourselves with such a clear lens, but you've taught me I need to do that. I'm thankful for the work your mom has done to awaken both of us. I miss your mom, Aunt Michele, so much and know she is looking down on you prouder than ever.

My Grandparents: Nan and Pop. I'm so lucky to still have you in my life. Pop S., you always taught me to set goals and have dreams. Nan, you always made my friends and I feel safe and at home whenever I would come and visit. You also make the best mashed potatoes on the planet. Thank you for ALL you do for my family and me. Syd and Saige are so lucky to have their great-grandparents in their lives!

Nan and Pop Peters: Although you are no longer here, you raised me to be the person I am today. I miss you every day, but I know you are always with me.

Extended family: I have so many aunts, uncles, cousins, etc. that I cannot possibly name here, but please know that without you, I would not be where I am today. We have shared memories or lessons that have shaped my life. I love you all!

Jay: My dear friend, without you, this book may never have been written. You introduced me to *The Secret* and gave me the title of this book. I am forever grateful that Ed met you and brought not only us, but our families together. Goddaughter Kaya and Navah are such blessings. Our conversations around spirituality shaped not only this book, but my life in so many ways. Now we have Ed as a reminder that love never dies, and we are always connected.

My Treasure Tribe:

Allie: I'll never forget that day I met you. It was during the Freshmen Walk at Etown. I shouted out that I was looking for a running partner and you responded! We only got to spend a semester together before you transferred thanks to Smartie candies (did that really happen?!); however, the Universe knew that was not the end. It was only the beginning. I'm so grateful Facebook kept us connected, and you reached out when I posted about synchronicities. From that moment on, we began calling and texting almost every day. You are an actual angel on this Earth, and I am convinced the Universe has used you as an instrument to aid me on my spiritual path.

Amy (or as my family knows you Reiki Amy): I only met you a few years ago in a Facebook group yet, I feel like you could be my twin flame. When I met you, my life felt whole and complete at last. Your incredible ability to heal has transformed me on a spiritual and emotional level that years of therapy never did. I love you and your soul.

Donna: I'm forever grateful that Allie introduced us! Thank you for the writing tips and your guidance around this book. More importantly, I love and appreciate your willingness to offer healing and love anytime my family or I need it. Your words of encouragement and advice are always so eloquently articulated. Although I've never had the pleasure of meeting you in person (yet), I feel like I have known you forever.

My Pennsylvania Tribe:

Steph, Lori, Ericka, Shauna: Miles may separate us, but it will never separate our friendship. We have shared so many good and bad times over the decades. You always have my back and love me even when I am unlovable. Your support and friendship is a gift I cherish and never take for granted. I cannot thank you enough for all you have done for my family and me. I love and miss you so much and look forward to many more adventures together.

Duarte and Thriller: Dance and drama connected our friendship. Oh, the stories we can share about the mess! You two got me through some very dark days but gave me many laughs, too. I always loved dance, and Thriller, you awakened that part of me that had gone to sleep. Duarte, you helped me to grow as a teacher, coach, and person. Thank you for allowing me to also help both of you in your journeys. Duarte, I am so proud of your transformation!

Jocelyn: I wish I had known you in high school, because it would have given me more time to spend with you. Although, I have to trust that the Universe connected us in Divine timing. I appreciate all of the healing you have given to my mom and me. I appreciate you opening up your home to me, too. I am looking forward to our retreat here in Hawai'i and serving our soul sisters. You're a beautiful soul; I'm so blessed to have you walking me home.

Mrs. Frezeman: Although you began as my ninth-grade English teacher, you have become a mentor, mother figure, and dear friend. While you taught me many quotes, I can still recite; you taught me about life. You taught me to keep your body and mind strong, which is why you can live on your own at ninety-three-years-young! Through your handwritten letters and cards, you taught me to celebrate every moment in life. To be grateful for everything, even if it is something as small as a blade of grass. "A thing of beauty is a joy forever..."

Mrs. Naffin: Latin was one of my favorite classes! I chose to take up to Level 5 because *you* were my teacher. I have such beautiful memories of your class, especially the Latin Convention at Penn State. I still can't believe you convinced me to run for State Secretary, but I loved that experience! Thank you so much for your help with the "Decide" chapter, and for being an inspiring teacher and friend.

The Cieslak Family: Steph, you were in my first class when I began teaching. You introduced me to your parents Lisa and Joe and years later I was partying with all of you at POTN! Because of your Groupon find, my brother and I got to go skydiving! Next up: New Orleans!

Catie: I am so grateful you were my student all those years ago. I'm so grateful your mom took me up on my offer to connect. You are a big sister to Syd and Saige, not just their first babysitter. I am beyond proud of the teacher and woman you have become. Your students are so lucky to have you as their teacher, but I am the luckiest to have you as part of our family.

Katrina and Jill: My gurlz! Despite having moved halfway around the planet, when I come back to PA for a visit, it's as if we never missed a beat. So glad we met as colleagues and became dear friends!

Karen: My travel buddy and roomie. We started out connected as middle-level educators serving on PAMLE. Still, those long (sometimes snowy) car rides across Pennsylvania made us fast friends. It seemed like an unlikely friendship to some because of our age difference. However, the more we got to know each other, the more we realized we were both on a spiritual journey. You saved me from taking a job that wasn't right for me and showed me to trust in Divine timing.

George Withers: Your psychic readings over the past few years have given me clarity on my life and purpose. You predicted my move to Hawai'i and told me I would write three books. So it looks like I have one down and two to go! Although you have predicted many other events that have come to fruition, I do know I have free will. The only limits are the ones I impose upon myself.

My Sisters and Brothers around the USA:

Carolyn: my BFF! I'll never forget that day in seventh grade home ec class when I saw this gorgeous blonde with big blue eyes share a smile with me. Over the years, we have made some incredible memories. Your mom introduced me to God and took me to church, the same church I had been baptized in. Amazing how God wanted me back. Through the years, I learned about my spirituality between games on the Ouija board, making bread, and writing letters to Jill Eikenberry and Michael Tucker. When you moved to California, I was worried our friendship would change. It sure did, but it only made us stronger. Moving to Hawai'i actually gave me more chances to visit you and Tabs. While I don't mention Christianity in this book, please know that if it hadn't been for meeting you and your family, I am not sure I would know God and Jesus. You were the angel he sent so I could find God again.

Jeremy: I met you in seventh grade and although it started out as a crush on my end (have I actually ever told you that??? LOL), you became my best guy friend and brother. We made some amazing memories from dirty dancing together in ninth grade chorus, Latin class antics, fun times terrorizing your brother (sorry, Greg), and late nights at Eat 'n Park.

Irene: You are the best person to happen to Jer. You've given him those gorgeous girls, Phi and Sasha. We can never thank you for opening up your home to us when we needed help. Not only did you provide a warm place to sleep, you comforted us in times of immense grief. Thank you will never suffice, so you need to get to Hawai'i so we can repay you!

Chris: You began as our neighbor and became an integral part of the family. I am most grateful for the years you babysat Syd and Saige and helped them grow into the young women they are today. We love Miss Chris and Madison! Thank you for trusting me; you were my first official client! You were with me as I wrote each page of this book. I'm looking forward to visiting you and the kids at your beach house someday soon.

Robin, my wack snake soul sister: We've come a long way since those days at E-town. Don't worry, I will not and certainly not, reveal any of those secrets. I'm just grateful that despite being in different classes, we remained soul sisters. I still can't believe we talk almost every Sunday and have for the past few decades! It's proof that people can make time for what matters. We have been through some shizz but always come out stronger. I admire your strength and resilience and all you do to serve humanity.

Stacy: My spiritual running buddy! It's incredible how my biggest "competition" many years ago has become one of my best teachers and supporters. I have learned so much from you about teaching, parenting, and spirituality. Together we have grown and evolved taking turns lifting each other up. It's been a wild journey so far; I can't wait to see what lies ahead for both of us.

Lisa G: Thank God for KU and grad school; otherwise, I would not have met one of the brightest lights and talented teachers on this planet. You may be years younger than me, but I will never forget the profound advice you gave me when I began freaking out about moving to Hawai'i. "Just because you make one choice, doesn't mean you can't make another." You went first by moving and creating a beautiful life and fulfilling career. You are a blessing to all who know you. Those students are so lucky to have you as their teacher. Keep modeling and proving to them that they can make their dreams come true; you are proof!

The Algeo Family: Shannon, I'm so grateful I found your unicorn group and *you*! This practice has profoundly changed my life! I love that we shared a moment on FB live. Mama Algeo and Michael, I'm so grateful I got to meet you and spend time with you in Hawai'i.

Our Hawaiian ʻOhana:
Zack and Kevin (The Guncles): There are people you meet who profoundly change you and you are never the same. I cannot believe we haven't known you our whole lives because I feel like we've spent lifetimes together. I am not sure we would have made it in Hawai'i had we not met you on that first day. What you have done for my family and me can never be repaid; I know you would never expect it. Thank you for being the best Hawaiian Uncles to the girls and our brothers from another mother. There are no words to express how much I love and adore you both.

The Tom ʻOhana: You were the first family in Hawai'i to show us the true meaning of aloha. You are not just our dear friends, but you have become our ʻOhana. There are not enough words in the English language to express how incredibly blessed we are to know such a selfless, kind, and generous family. We look forward to many more Weaver/Tom get-togethers!

Sydni, Guilia, Olivia, & Gabs: You would literally and figuratively drive the entire island for us. We are forever grateful that you opened your home and heart to Saige. You gave her space where she feels supported and safe to be her authentic self. I cherish our conversations, whether they be over wine, on the phone, or in a text.

The Brands: THANK YOU! For everything. Especially your willingness to help us in Hawai'i and NYC during a very difficult time in our lives. It meant the world to us that you invited Sydney to spend a week with your family. It was an experience she will never forget. Malindi, thank you for always offering an ear, a shoulder, or a glass of wine; I appreciate your friendship.

Mel: Good lord, I've only known you only for a few years, but I *know* I've known you for lifetimes. I don't think it was the one with dinosaurs, but I digress. I truly don't know what to type because how do you thank the person that's lifted you up, supported you, listened to you, and loved you when you didn't always deserve one minute of it? I have never met someone who is so kind and generous with their heart and love. You should be the definition of aloha. PS. You should also be the definition of hugs; you give the best ones!

Theresa: I was your "replacement," although let's be clear, no one could ever replace you. Then the Universe laughed and said, "Nope, you two are destined to meet, so surprise... she's coming back!" You and I have also had some lifetimes together. You've taught me so much about my own spirituality and how to tap into my intuitive powers. Although we both have undergone some powerful lessons, you've taught me to wear that shit like a boss. I love that you are fierce and feminine. Don't mess with these spiritual warriors!

Lisa Anne: SIS! Omg! I love you. I love how you *love* being a teacher and mother. You give, and give, and give to everyone and everything you love. Your passion and enthusiasm are contagious! You model the aloha spirit in your words, deeds, and actions. Thank you for always making me feel like I am a part of you and your 'Ohana.

Kings & Ku My Hawaiian brothers: *Mahalo Nui Loa* for your willingness to teach this *Haole* Hawaiian culture and language. I could not have written that chapter without your help. More importantly, thank you for showing me the true meaning of aloha. Kings: Because of you, we have JERB! I love you, *more*!

Aldene: I cannot thank you enough for your time, wisdom, and help with my last chapter. You are my birthday twin and soul sister. I know we have spent lifetimes together here in Hawai'i. I'm so grateful the Universe allowed me to remember this lifetime with you.

Michelle: You are the "best partner in crime." Thank you for putting up with me. You are so patient and forgiving. I appreciate all of the gifts you give the girls and me, especially the ones you've handmade. I don't tell you enough how much I appreciate you. When I look around at other relationships, I realize how incredibly lucky we are. We may be so different in so many ways, but it works. I couldn't imagine doing SAO without you!

Jen & Martin: Thank you for opening up your home to us on Maui. Spending time with you there or in Oahu is always fun. Jen, thanks for taking me to walk on Oprah's road. We had some deep conversations, and I value your advice and wisdom.

Karen N: The move to Hawai'i would not have been possible without all of your help. Your willingness to go to the apartment we had found and Facetime us in, so we could have a place to live, speaks volumes to the type of person you are. If it weren't for you, Scott wouldn't have gotten the job. Thank you for trusting me to cat sit. It was during that time, I knew unequivocally, I needed to write this book.

Joline: You were the first Aunty to help my family and me those early days when we first arrived in Hawai'i. I'll also never forget the fantastic car ride we shared on the way to my interview. *Mahalo* for showing us aloha professionally and personally.

T-Wong: Thank you for taking my beautiful website photos and for your artistic eye and guidance on the cover and book design.

My 'Iolani 'Ohana: I'm blessed to work with the most amazing colleagues. For fear I may miss someone, I'm not going to list any names, but you know who you are.

Amy (or neighbor Amy): When we first moved into our condo, you were there to offer anything we needed. But what I remember most is your beautiful smile. Thank you for becoming a friend and a spiritual soul sister.

Lizz: Without you my hair would never look amazing! You're a talented hairstylist and even better "therapist". If the chair could talk, we'd both be in trouble!

My Mentors:

Christy Whitman: Because of you and the Quantum Success Coaching Academy, I became a certified Law of Attraction Coach. More importantly, I learned a lot about myself and how much inner work I still needed to do. Your program was by far the best investment I have ever made in myself and broke me open to healing the wounds that have plagued me for decades. I need to also acknowledge that most of what I write in this book, I learned from you. You taught me how to use the spiritual laws so I could manifest my life in paradise.

Rachel: I'm so grateful you were my teacher during my program in the QSCA. You are one of the sweetest and kindest souls I have been blessed to know. I'm so glad we could be friends all these years later.

Sarah: You were my first business coach who helped me get content up for my website and taught me that I was a coach before I wanted to wear the title. I am forever grateful that you introduced me to Vanessa.

Vanessa Simpkins: Without you and your company *Take Your Power Back Now* (TYPBN), I would not have a coaching business or a book! Your program not only taught me business strategies but helped me reprogram limiting beliefs and change my mindset. Then you allowed me to work with you and your fantastic team as a mindset mentor. My favorite memory is eating Italian takeout and dancing with you and Freedom in your living room. That night, I went back to my hotel and cried happy tears because I realized a manifestation had come true. I came to know you on a FB ad webinar and said, I'm going to meet and work with her, and it happened! I'm also grateful for the time we shared in Hawai'i and meeting Alex. Because of you, I met Les and could finally get this book birthed!

The Team at TYPBN: I am so grateful to be surrounded by empowering, strong women. We are the dream team and every day I am inspired by the lives we change and the profound impact this team is making on women throughout the world. A special shoutout to my mindset team: Kimberly, Penni, and Nicci; I love you ladies beyond words.

Les, the book coach: Without you, this book would still be stuck in my head. You've given me the guidance, motivation, and at times, a swift kick in the ass to get my chapters written. You started as someone I hired to write a book and have become a trusted friend. I can't wait to write the next one with you.

Sybil, Indigo Alliance: Thank you for allowing me to promote my book and teach at your impressive center. I'm so grateful I found this spiritual home and was welcomed so warmly by you and your staff. I love the classes and all I have learned and am honored now that I can share my teachings.

My clients: Thank you to *all* of you. Your trust in me is the best gift I could ever receive. I'm proud of you for saying *yes* to yourselves and learning how to live the life you were born to live!

Manifesting Miracles Facebook group: Initially, I started that group for my coaching business, but it has become so much more. I love the tribe and community we've created. Thank you for your guidance in writing this book. Remember: you can create miracles!

My former and current students: I became a teacher to make a positive difference in the lives of my students. I got much more than I bargained for. You have made a profound difference in my life and an indelible handprint on my heart.

My guides, angels, ascended masters, and Source: It took me a long time to know and accept you. You tried to get my attention many times; I ignored you. I apologize for our years of separation. Your lessons have awakened me to my mission. Thank you for guiding me back to myself and wholeness, and allowing me to live my purpose so that I can help others live their own aloha.

CPSIA information can be obtained
at www.ICGtesting.com
Printed in the USA
BVHW092053281022
650569BV00006B/226

9 781525 582158